GARDENS UNDER
BIG SKIES

GARDENS UNDER BIG SKIES

REIMAGINING OUTDOOR SPACE, THE DUTCH WAY

Noel Kingsbury
Maayke de Ridder

GARDENS UNDER BIG SKIES

The original edition was published in Dutch by Noordboek | HL Books under the title Van landschap naar tuin
© 2021 Noel Kingsbury & Maayke de Ridder / Noordboek | HL Books
info@hlbooks.nl

This edition published in 2021 by Filbert Press Ltd
© English edition 2021 Noel Kingsbury & Maayke de Ridder / Filbert Press

Concept: Hélène Lesger and Maayke de Ridder
Photography: Maayke de Ridder
Design: Alan Watt

A catalogue record for this book is available from the British Library
ISBN 978-1-9997345-9-6

Printed by Printer Trento S.r.l., Italy

GARDENS UNDER BIG SKIES

FOREWORD

Noel Kingsbury first came to visit us in Hummelo in 1994. He returned frequently over the next few years, and along the way we started to write together. His interest in what I was doing was part of a wider project he was engaged with, looking at new and mostly nature-inspired planting in gardens and landscapes. At that time – the early to mid-1990s – we were rebellious, doing something new and wanting to create our own world. The people working with perennials and wild flowers in The Netherlands all knew each other, met up during special plant weekends, and also attended a series of annual conferences that were running at the time – Perennial Perspectives. Noel became part of our group of 'plants people', and during this period he got to know us all: Rob Leopold in Groningen, Leo den Dulk in Arnhem, Henk Gerritsen at the Priona Gardens, Coen Jansen in Dalfsen, Hein Koningen who oversaw the parks management at Amstelveen, and other specialist growers.

Our ideas, like our plants, grew, spread and multiplied. This book is partly about that multiplication that saw the use of plants that were once a minority interest among gardeners became almost mainstream – especially the wild plants in wild places that Henk, in particular, had a passion for and which are now part of the culture for many garden people. The book also shows how the influences of the past shape our present, such as that of Mien Ruys, a designer who so dominated Dutch garden and landscape design that it felt difficult to escape her influence. Now a new generation is rediscovering her and reinterpreting her ideas for our time.

This book is also about our country and landscape. Clearly the country was getting under Noel's skin – even if he did complain about how easy it was to get lost as everywhere looked the same! After a while he began to learn to read the landscape and appreciate that it is much more diverse than people often think, and in this book he looks at how it forms part of the background for the work of the new generation of garden and landscape designers.

Learning to read the landscape takes time and not all visitors do that. This book is the outcome not just of garden visiting and talking to designers, but patient observation of a lot more too.

Piet Oudolf

INTRODUCTION

Holland or, more accurately, The Netherlands, is flat – famously so. This means the skies are big and perspectives are inevitably very different from those of landscapes with more elevation. But gardens are shaped by history as well as geography, and in the case of The Netherlands, that history was one driven, as it was for all of Europe up until some time in the 18th century, by the formal garden, a style of Italian inspiration (rather than origin, as it could well be argued that this particular form of garden first appeared in Persia) that arrived in Italy via the classical civilizations of Greece and Rome. Geography decreed that Dutch gardens were almost inevitably going to be flat, and since geometric formality is a very good way of organizing and giving meaning to space, providing sight lines and a sense of perspective, the combination of formality and flatness worked together rather well. Geography also decreed a frequent necessity for canals and other bodies of water, and necessity being the mother of invention, organizing water became something of a passion for Dutch garden-makers.

Gardens are often a reaction to the wider landscape. They tend to domesticate and idealize, and sometimes seek to miniaturize, the landscape that surrounds the garden-maker, or in some cases, more distant landscapes that for one reason or other the garden-maker regards as worthy of emulation. Here we look at some contemporary Dutch gardens as the product of a unique cultural landscape. Some of them are very consciously about reinterpreting elements of that landscape for the garden; others do quite the opposite, looking beyond its obvious limitations to hillier and rockier places. For the most part they reflect and reinterpret elements of their surroundings in many subtle ways.

Those features of the Dutch landscape that set it apart from others are largely artificial, the product of the human hand rather than natural process, although the flatness and the big skies are inevitable – nature's drawing board for human imagination. To understand the landscape background to Dutch gardens we need to know something of the country itself, which means having some understanding of how these landscape features that make it unique came to be.

As is so often the case, the end of the last Ice Age is a good place to start – in time, that is. And place? Schipol Airport seems logical. It is, after all, how a great many foreign visitors arrive. But the airport is also a very good location to start thinking about the interplay between history and geography that defines this country's landscape, for this was once the centre of a sizeable lake, the Haarlemmermeer – not just any lake, but one that was very large, dangerously unstable and threatening to rip the heart out of the country. An expression was used to describe lakes that ate away at their banks and continually enlarged: *waterwolf*. The Haarlemmermeer was the ultimate waterwolf.

At the end of the Ice Age, today's Netherlands was more or less in the middle of a vast low, swampy plain that went from today's Denmark right across to what is now England's Yorkshire. As the ice melted most of this flooded, leaving a tract of land jutting gently out from north-west Europe that acted as the delta of various rivers, most notably the Rhine, which drains a huge area from Switzerland northwards. The stabilization of the sea-level allowed this land's coastline to settle too, more or less, largely through a great arc of sand dunes which protected the land from the sea. Today's visitor may find it hard to believe that the historic province of Holland, now the densely populated core of the country, was once desolate swamp,

moorland and, at best, poor grazing land. The parts of 'the low countries' which started to develop during medieval times were south of this, among the islands and peninsulas of the delta region, today's Zeeland, where the rivers Rhine, Meuse and Scheldt emerge into the sea; or they were in the north and east, in what came to be known as Friesland, where the monasteries played an important role in developing land for farming and settlement, as they did in many other parts of Europe.

Back to that arc of sand dunes. Anyone looking at a map will see that the Dutch coast sweeps north from the Delta area and then curves round so that it ends up being nearly at a right angle to its starting point. At the top end, towards Germany, the solid line of the coast is broken, but is followed by a series of islands. Only a little imagination is required to realize that these islands are the remnants of a coastline which existed in the past – they were part of the wall of sand dunes that defines the coastline. Sand seems a strangely insubstantial element to stand up to the sea, especially a sea emboldened by a raging winter storm; our minds stretch back to childhood sand castles on the beach. However, when the sandy seabed was exposed at low tide, the sun and the wind dried it out, so the sand was blown away to drop inland to form the dunes. Summers saw grasses, wild flowers, even shrubs and trees, begin to grow and consolidate the sand and to trap yet more wind-blown sand. So, over millennia, grew the dunes – one of the few natural interruptions of that perfect hemisphere of sky.

From the medieval period onwards, an overriding concern regarding the two most populated regions – today's Zeeland and Friesland – was draining the land and then protecting it from further flooding. To this end, a progressively sophisticated system of dykes – embankments to keep

At the end of the Ice Age, today's Netherlands was more or less in the middle of a vast low, swampy plain that went from today's Denmark right across to what is now England's Yorkshire.

01

01
The ever-extending coastline: the sea eating its way into the territory covered by The Netherlands over the last 2000 years, mainly through the growth of the Zuiderzee.

01

In 1282, a huge storm broke through the sand dunes on the coast, near what is now the island of Texel, while a few years later, in 1287, another storm surge drowned at least 50,000 people, one of the worst floods in European history.

01
Dorkwerd, in Groningen province – a terp village, with its church on the highest point and the mound clearly visible.

02
A riddle in the landscape? A Zeeland mound where medieval villagers could flee floods or enemies.

03
The Saint Elizabeth's Day flood, painted by an anonymous artist in the early 1490s, some 70 years after the disaster.

04
The Verdronken Land van Saeftinghe – the 'drowned land', a continuing legacy of the All Saints' Day Flood of 1 November 1570.

the water out of the fields – was invented. These also made it easier to remove water from defined areas, so draining the land. For the most part, every piece of land gained that was dry enough for farmers to grow crops or graze cattle or sheep was a victory won through sheer hard work; a flood or storm could destroy the labour of years in a matter of hours. Not only were dykes required to protect from high tides pushing water inland from river mouths, they were also vital to prevent land from drowning when the rivers flooded as a result of high rainfall. A village's dykes also had to hold back the increasing amounts of water that were being redirected away from neighbouring communities too. Indeed, the growing population and settlement meant that communities increasingly had to co-ordinate their drainage schemes to avoid flooding each other; the complex system of water boards that exist today had its roots in these early efforts.

In those distant times, people not surprisingly tried to live on higher ground, so that if there was a flood, they, their goods and their livestock could be safe. Any little bit of elevation could be raised, again with patient digging and the banging in of pales to contain soil – even the manure from the livestock helped. These were the *terpen* (singular *terp*). The core of many a village, especially in Friesland, but also in Zeeland (and even in Flanders and Denmark) is one of these mounds, often occupied partly by a church. Further south, the Delta region had a larger population than the coastal province of Holland and was considerably more developed. The landscape can reflect this; with bumps and hollows, areas around villages can point to centuries of small-scale dyke building or the local equivalent of the terp, the *vliedbergen*.

And so, slowly, the dykes were built out further and built up, and more land was drained. However, there was a big problem, one that was in fact self-inflicted. Like someone sitting on the branch of a tree busily cutting it off, while sitting on the wrong side, the late medieval Dutch population was making its marginal situation against the waters even more perilous. The reason for this was peat, and the nature of this deposit which covered, and indeed still covers, large areas. The result of a partial, or only minimal, decomposition of plant matter in waterlogged and therefore anaerobic conditions, peat is a dark, spongy material. Dry it out and it shrinks, by as much as five times. Drainage canals cut through peat

result in the surface drying out and sinking, making it more vulnerable to flooding.

The fact that dried peat was a good fuel was another reason to drain the land where it was found. By itself this would not have been too bad, but this already vulnerable land fed an important industry that made the problem far worse – salt production. Salt was a valuable commodity in pre-industrial Europe, vital for preserving food, and was traded over long distances. The climate precluded drying out seawater in the sun, as happened in southern European salt pans, so boiling in giant kettles was used instead, fuelled by peat – vast quantities of it.

As the peatlands shrank, so the land level dropped, exacerbating the slow post-glacial rise in sea level. A particular weak spot was the Zuiderzee, an arm of the sea which divided Friesland (to the east) from the land to the west. What had been a lake during Roman times gradually became salt water, as storms and rising seas ate away at its shores. In 1282, a huge storm broke through the sand dunes on the coast, near what is now the island of Texel, while a few years later, in 1287, another storm surge drowned at least 50,000 people, one of the worst floods in European history. As an arm of the sea, the new Zuiderzee enabled ships to reach Amsterdam, helping to start the city's inexorable rise, but opened up

02

a huge geographical weakness, allowing storm-driven seas to work their way into the land from behind the defensive line of coastal dunes, which were gradually being reduced to a chain of sandy islands.

On November 19, 1421, St Elizabeth's Day, a storm in the North Sea led to a tidal surge which overwhelmed some poorly maintained dykes in the south. Several thousand people died and around 70 villages are thought to have been lost; the city of Dordrecht, one of the most important trading ports in the region, became stranded as an island. Some of the land which was flooded has never been reclaimed. Other floods in this period, usually named after the saint's days on which they occurred, took more land. The St Felix flood of 1530 drowned large parts of Zeeland, killing many more than the better-known St Elizabeth Day event, part of its legacy today being the Verdronken Land van Reimerswaal – the drowned land of Reimerswaal – while the result of the All Saints Day flood of 1570 was the loss of several islands; this lives on as the Verdronken land van Saeftinghe, now a nature reserve with myriad small channels running through salt marsh.

03

The historical trauma of the St Elizabeth Day flood submerged some 300 sq km (116 sq miles) of polder land, much of which has never been fully reclaimed. Known as the Biesbosch, this is now one of the largest areas of tidal freshwater marshland in Europe, and a major national park. Some areas are farmed, mostly as rough grazing, while the area covered by the national park is a landscape of willow and reeds, often impenetrable except by boat. Travelling around the Biesbosch in this way is a fascinatingly exotic experience, like a temperate version of the Louisiana swamps.

Partly this is the result of a reduced tidal influence, so water levels are more stable, which has led to willow beginning to take over from reeds across much of the area.

The fight-back against rising water levels took a turn with the development of windmills, which began to be used from the late 13th century onwards. By the birth of the Dutch Republic in 1581, they were pumping vast quantities of water out of canals, enabling more land to be reclaimed – the polders – and safeguarding that which was already present. From now on, a number of technologies worked in step, all of them with an impact on the landscape: windmills to remove water, bigger and stronger dykes to keep water out, polder-creation to drain land and canal-digging to keep water moving. A key change in the appearance of the land must have been the draining of lakes, which were not just of little use, but positively dangerous, as many had low, weak sides which could be eaten away by storms – the 'water wolves'.

Windmills could only do so much, however. The Zuiderzee remained dangerous and by the late 19th century it threatened to join up with the Haarlemmermeer, which as a large body of shallow water was liable to particularly dangerous shifting and surging in a storm, each storm potentially resulting in metres of shoreline eaten away. In the early 16th century it, and three smaller lakes, had a surface area of around 26 sq km (10 sq miles), but by the mid-17th century it was one lake of 66 sq km (25 sq miles). A storm brought its waters to the gates of Amsterdam in 1836. Steam-powered pump technology arrived just in time and by 1852 it was dry, thanks to the construction of a ring dyke to drain it and then the creation of polders. It is now the site of Schipol Airport.

Having gained confidence in defending their land and adding to it, Dutch engineers grew increasingly ambitious, and in the 20th century set their sights on the Zuiderzee itself. Dammed, enclosed and tamed, it is now the more placid IJsselmeer. This was a turning point however, as plans to drain the entire body of water were never implemented, nor were even more ambitious plans to take on the Waddenzee to the north. The fact is that the ambitions of engineers were contested for much of the 20th century. Fishermen who needed access to the sea protested over the damming of the Zuiderzee and parts of the 1950s and 1960s Delta project in Zeeland, while from the 1960s onwards a growing

04

environmental movement has opposed many new projects.

If the Zuiderzee project was taking the offensive against nature, the Delta Works in the province of Zeeland which took place from the 1950s to the 1990s was defensive. A disastrous flood in 1953 hit the region around the combined estuaries of the Rhine, Meuse and Scheldt rivers, killing thousands. Since then, thanks to the nation's engineers, almost no-one has died in a flood. The Delta Works was essentially about shortening the coastline, so that dykes did not have to be extended along rivers. Some of the river mouths were shut, turning the areas behind them into freshwater or brackish lakes; others were protected by storm-surge barriers with enormous gates that can be shut when high tides threaten.

Unlike the Zuiderzee Works which largely proceeded according to plan, the Delta Works was subject to several changes, partly as a result of technological advances but also because of the opposition of environmentalists and fishing communities to some of the barrages. The conflict between the engineer and the naturalist which had begun in the 1930s with an early conservation movement was now played out for high stakes. Certain compromises were made to preserve certain habitats, most of them saltwater. Crucially, from 2006 the Dutch government has subscribed to 'Room for the River', an approach to flood management that aims at developing a more nature-friendly approach, with an emphasis on allowing flood waters to be retained in some areas. Some farmland has had to be sacrificed, and even some polders are allowed to occasionally flood, or

05

The conflict between the engineer and the naturalist has been played out, albeit in softer style, in domestic and community-managed gardens. Those passionate about nature have made wild gardens, mostly using native species, and designed to support as much animal life as possible.

05
Reeds and poplar forest in the Biesbosch. Once common, this type of wet forest is now very rare in Europe.

06
Part of the Delta Works project – giant barriers to prevent storm and tidal surges from flooding inland.

07
A *wipmolen* (seesaw mill) of 1735, in the Marendijkpolder near Gouda – a type of windmill used here for drainage.

have been returned to natural wetlands – policies that would have seemed anathema to previous generations. The new policy may be driven by a pragmatic need to temporarily hold water, and therefore makes good engineering sense, but the outcome can be to re-create spaces for nature.

The conflict between the vision of the engineer and that of the naturalist has bubbled into the open a good many times over the last three-quarters of a century. The engineer's vision of the country as a totally managed risk-free environment is not one that everyone wants or accepts, especially since it seems to have no room for curves, ripples, or rough or uneven bits – nothing in the landscape which is not measurable and quantifiable. Many people want some old houses, ancient trees and occasional unkempt areas of riverside, some even passionately so. The engineer's vision of control is one that suits the agricultural industry. The Netherlands has the world's most efficient systems of agriculture and is one of the biggest exporters of food, an incredible fact given its small size. Lovers of nature will point out that this has been achieved through the intensive use of fertilizers and herbicides that eliminate all plant species other than the farmers' crops, and a government-backed programme of farm consolidation which rationalizes farm boundaries to make them more efficient. It is not surprising that many find this accountancy-led management of the countryside quite abhorrent.

As the political influence of the nature lobby increased, something interesting began to happen, as 'new nature' began to become part of the planning process. Planners for farm consolidations began to recognize the areas of biodiversity about to be eliminated and arranged for new wild areas to be created as compensation. More initiatives were taken. Roadsides began to be cut later, allowing more wild flowers to bloom, and 'habitat creation' took off, usually involving the sowing of wild flower seed mixes in places such as housing areas, industrial estates and highway interchanges where only grass might have been seen before. Oostvaardersplassen, an area reclaimed from the Zuiderzee in 1968, has become not just a nature reserve but also the site of one of the world's leading projects in rewilding, allowing natural processes to take over with minimal management, including the introduction of wild animals such as primitive breeds of horse and cattle.

To the outsider, all of this looks quite encouraging. The engineers may still have the upper hand, but those who fight nature's corner now have a voice that in the past they were not granted. The conflict between the engineer and the naturalist has been played out, albeit in softer style, in domestic and community-managed gardens. Those passionate about nature have made wild gardens, mostly using native species, and designed to support as much animal life as possible. The organization Oase stages events in support of nature-friendly gardening on an impressive scale. Yet a drive around the average suburb reveals, for the most part, a love of gardening which involves showy plants and total control, like a miniature and artistic version of the engineered landscape. The gardens in this book take something from both

06

approaches, as many of them incorporate elements of sustainability or wildness or at least an aesthetic which is a long way from the foaming masses of *Hydrangea* 'Annabelle' with a neat box border so often seen. A legacy from millennia of land-shaping, however, informs much of the contemporary design creativity. Order and nature here at least seem to have found some sort of resolution. The Biesbosch and the Oostvaardersplassen are two examples of how the Dutch attempts to control nature have come full circle. Both represent a compromise in the battle between the engineers of nature and those who would rather let nature take its course. On a smaller scale, a great many gardeners have reached similar compromises in their own gardens.

GARDENS UNDER BIG SKIES

INSPIRED BY NATURAL LANDSCAPES

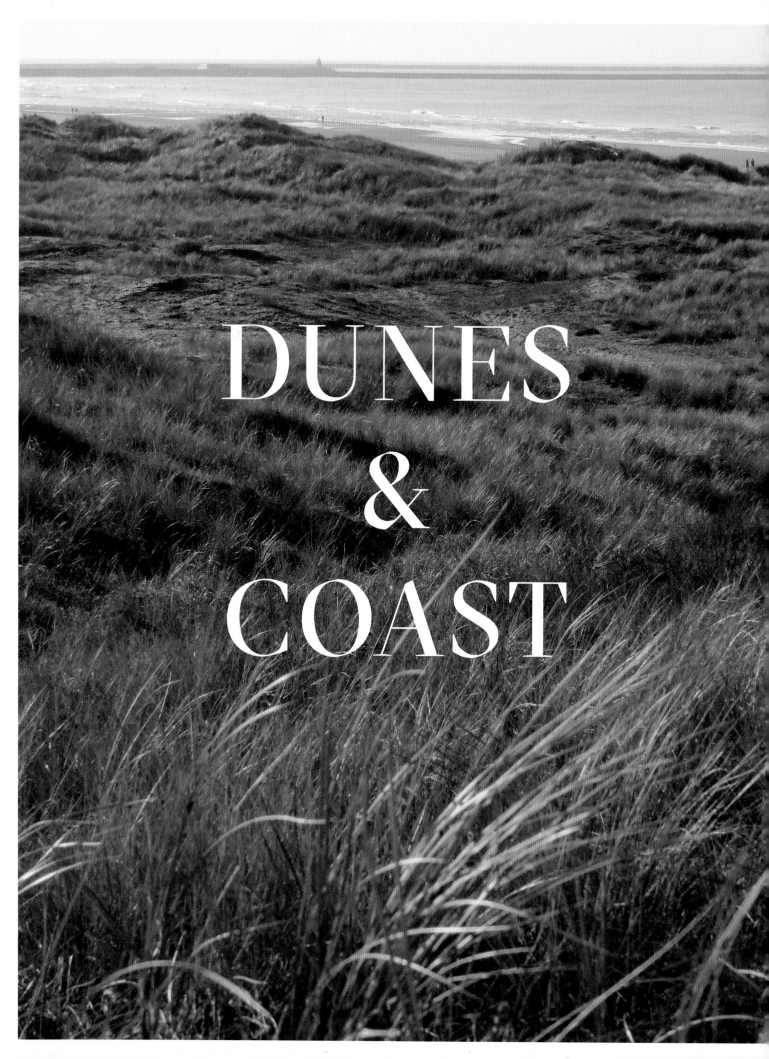

DUNES
&
COAST

'Walking down to the sea' is a phrase that resonates through the literatures or expressions of many cultures. The sea is always down from the land, dramatically so for those who live on rocky coasts, less so perhaps for those whose shorelines do not involve much elevation, but nevertheless always down. The first sight of the sea is always a crucial moment in any journey to the coast, and this first glimpse is often from afar and very often from height.

The Dutch coastline by comparison often involves the paradox of first having to go up, either because the land is below sea-level or if not, between 'dry land' and the sea there is a barrier of sand dunes, which require a climb up before it is possible to then walk down to the shoreline. The sea is rarely seen until it is right in front of you. It does not reveal itself gradually like it does to other nations; an awareness of it comes suddenly, as you turn a corner or come down from a gentle slope. Few things emphasize more powerfully that this is a land below the waters. The sight of a wall of dunes with the knowledge that behind them lies the sea, at a higher level, is disconcerting, at least to the non-Dutch visitor. Where the dunes are replaced by a dyke, an inevitably narrower structure, the feeling of unease is even greater.

The Dutch coast is essentially a barrier of sand blown into dunes by the wind, a natural defence for the land behind. It's extraordinary that it carried on unbroken for so long and protected the land for centuries. Breaches in it, or weak points, threatened all on the other side. The medieval breach of the barrier in the north that created the Waddenzee and extended the Zuiderzee was a case in point. As well as breaches, the coastline has also been threatened by an endless succession of retreats; a decision to maintain it at the limits of 1990 necessitates much dredging and manipulation of currents to deposit sand where it helps to protect the coastline against storms.

A coast that is an effective barrier is also one that offers no safe harbours, so this particular one has tended to be very empty of settlement. Only the occasional beach-launched boat or people wading into the waters with nets offered opportunities for fishing. Little broke the immensely wide beaches of damp sand that stretched from the horizon behind to the horizon ahead. Harbours for fishing fleets were inevitably away from the coast itself, on calmer bodies of water behind the protective barrier of dunes. The same applied to trading ports, whose ships often had to sail for long and circuitous distances along inland waterways simply to get out to sea. The nation that built itself on trade often had a paradoxically difficult time of it actually getting to the waves.

The sand of the dunes creates a very special environment. The instability of the surface beneath the feet often means that a trek through the dunes feels like two steps forwards, one step back. Such a loose surface is difficult for plants too; the only survivors are those that can cope with frequent disruption, drought, salt spray and almost constant exposure to wind.

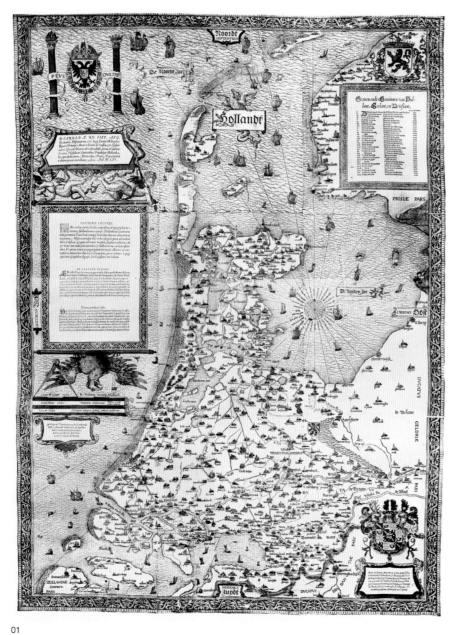

01

03

02

INSPIRED BY NATURAL LANDSCAPES

The sand is generally pale, and the plants that thrive (or survive) in it are pale too, their leaves often coated in a waxy layer that helps to reduce moisture loss, or protects against strong sunlight or abrasion. On a sunny day, this is a landscape that looks and feels bleached, drained of strong colours, a landscape of pale yellows, greys, dull greens. On an overcast day, when grey sky meets grey sea, colours are muted further.

Beyond the line of coastal dunes, the landscape is often dominated by sand. This is a most intriguing environment. There is a bit more colour (the dark greens of pines, for example) and often a rich wild flower flora but fundamentally this feels a world apart, the sound and the awareness of the sea disappearing behind high dunes frozen into immobility through their coating of grass. There is no sense of it being anywhere remotely recognizable as 'normal' land, Dutch or anywhere else. Dunescapes are fascinating environments, the vistas often changing dramatically from one bend in the path to another. Patches of scrubby poplars or willows appear among the grasses, become more woodland-like groves of oak or pine further inland, or may be replaced by impenetrable thickets of sea buckthorn or blackthorn – or more dramatically, by a sudden sea of loose sand. The skin of vegetation that keeps the sand in place is thin and ruptures easily, returning stable dunes to a wind-driven mobility.

    Above all, the landscape of the inner dunes has a random quality. The landscape most north Europeans are used to is one which is defined by a hierarchy of valleys as smaller streams flow into larger ones which flow into rivers; the hills left behind will usually be approximately similar in size and have roughly similar outlines and gradients. Of course this is not the case anywhere in The Netherlands apart from

01
A map of Holland in 1558, dominated by the Zuiderzee and its ports (now all inland). Note the substantial area covered by lakes.

02
Pinks (flat-bottomed fishing boats) in the surf, by Hendrik Willem Mesdag, c.1880. The catch is being divided after the ships have been hauled onto the beach.

03
Looking out over the dunes.

01

02

Limburg and the Utrechtse Heuvelrug, but it sets a kind of standard by which our subconscious reads the contours of a hilly landscape. Here in duneland, none of this holds good: the slopes and miniature hills of grass-encased sand appear to be random, there is no drainage pattern and, most disconcertingly, paths snake and braid, appear and disappear. It is all too easy to get lost. Compared to the engineered order of most of this country, this is an exhilaratingly different, challenging and sometimes disconcerting environment. There are no streams, as rainwater sinks straight into the sand, emerging only when the valleys between the dunes sink below the water table. The result is odd pools or areas of wet ground with a more luxuriant vegetation, sometimes even marshlands, all the more surreal for often being only metres away from dry sand. This ability of the sand to soak up water has been put to good use; as the water percolates down it is filtered and cleaned, making good drinking water. The city of Amsterdam gets its water from an area known as Panneland, where rainwater is gathered in rectangular ponds, percolated through sand and piped away.

03

At the centre of the largest area of dunes in the country woodland covers the inland portion before segueing into a unique savannah-like habitat before then turning to the more familiar grassy dunescape. The trees are familiar oaks and birch but they are set in a landscape that looks halfway to desert, the instability of the surface apparent from the sometimes bizarre angles of the tree trunks. This landscape may be a protective barrier for the land behind, but it is clearly one for which security can never be assured.

04

06

05

07

08

01
Sea holly (*Eryngium maritimum*) flourishes on sand dunes but has very particular requirements that make it reluctant to survive in most gardens except coastal ones.

02
The beach and the dunes at Wijk aan Zee; the sea is to the left.

03
Sea buckthorn (*Hippophae rhamnoides*), a tough dune plant with bright orange, Vitamin C-packed berries, also flourishes in Himalayan high-altitude deserts.

04
There are even some dune systems inland, almost unique in Europe.

05
Eventually woodland will replace the specialist dune flora, but it is typically very open and light, as here in North Holland Dune Reserve.

06
Sea buckthorn suckers to form dense colonies in time; with their branching and sharp spines, these are completely impenetrable.

07
Marram grass (*Ammophila arenaria*) is supremely adapted to survival in shifting sand, and helps to stabilize it over time.

08
The whole gradient of the ecological process of succession, from bare sand to woodland, can be seen here at Zuid-Kennemerland National Park.

INSPIRED BY NATURAL LANDSCAPES

01-02
Flowers of the dunes:
Beach rose (*Rosa rugosa*),
orange berries of sea
buckthorn (*Hippophae
rhamnoides*), marram
grass/sandweed
(*Ammophila arenaria*),
sea holly (*Eryngium
maritimum*), showy
stonecrop (*Sedum
telephium*), pinkish
common soapwort
(*Saponaria officinalis*),
blue-flowered alkanet
(*Anchusa officinalis*).

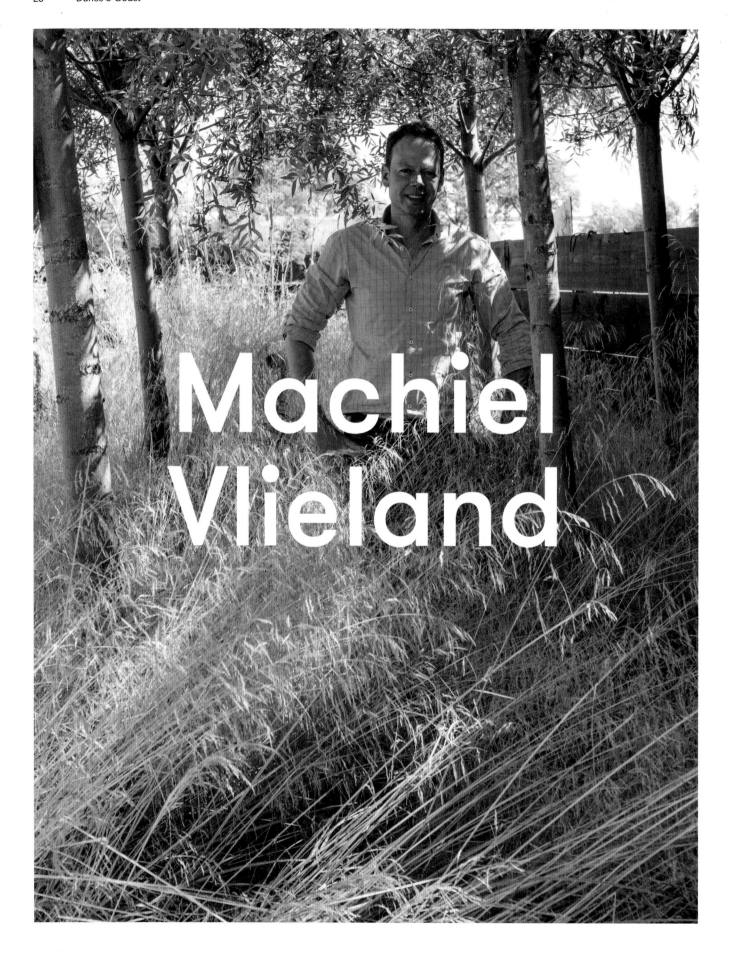

Machiel Vlieland

One of those children who loved growing things, Machiel Vlieland began taking cuttings and begging plants off neighbours when he was seven years old. 'My parents and grandparents gardened and I had always been fascinated by plants, but I had not really thought about gardening as a profession,' he says. 'But I didn't like school, I went on to business school and was expelled, so then I went to a horticulture school.' This was the Tuinbouwschool Huis te Lande in Rijswijk, which had originally been established as a college for girls in the 1910s, but from 1985 admitted boys and was amalgamated with another college in 2000. 'One of my teachers was Wim Oudshoorn, a famous plantsman of the 1980s,' recalls Machiel. 'We learned a lot about plants, although it was all quite old-fashioned.' Oudshoorn had indeed been a prolific writer on a wide variety of garden matters, with around 80 books published.

Machiel went on to study at the University of Larenstein near Arnhem for a year, but found it too abstract and mathematical for what he wanted to do. After leaving, he worked in garden centres for a number of years, before starting his own design office in 1997. He really broke the mould with a remarkable innovation, which like most great innovations made everyone else think 'Why didn't I do that?' He opened a tiny (18 sq m/22 sq yd) design studio in the city of Leiden, which acted as a 'design shop'. 'It was the first garden design shop in the country,' he says. 'I had drawings and photographs on display, so people could drop in and see what I could do. It was open three days a week from Thursday to Saturday, and when there was no-one in to talk to, I could work on a drawing board. It worked, and I have had progressively larger shops since then.'

A French friend suggested he call his business 'Extra Vert', a play on words that potentially covers everything green and implies that everything Machiel does goes beyond the everyday and essential. Since 2005 Machiel has worked with Marco Márquez as a business partner. With a marketing background, Marco was the ideal person to help in the shop, but the growing popularity of Extra Vert's garden designs led him to study garden design himself so that he could work with Machiel, dealing with clients and turning concepts into drawings that could then be used for implementation.

01
Sea buckthorn (*Hippophae rhamnoides*)
forms a dense shrub. There are male and
female plants, with berries only on the female.

02
Mexican feather grass (*Stipa tenuissima*),
a plant from the American south-west, has
become deservedly popular in gardens.

03
Santolina chamaecyparissus is a low-
growing Mediterranean shrub that is very
resistant to wind and salt exposure.

Machiel's growing business needed more and more space, and he moved to progressively larger premises until in 2013 he bought a semi-derelict building which now seems to be perfect for his needs. 'It was an old warehouse for flower bulbs, built in 1925. The local council charged us only for the land – the building was thrown in free, as we were willing to restore it. It's a good location, close to Leiden and Den Haag, and has enough space to develop a garden.'

Like many other Dutch designers, Machiel has travelled extensively to look at gardens, particularly to the UK. Among the places that have inspired him the most, he mentions Knoll Gardens in Dorset in southern England, where nursery owner Neil Lucas has an extensive collection of grasses well integrated with perennials. 'He is unique in his choice of plants,' he says. Others he rates highly are Scampston Hall, an early Piet Oudolf commission in northern England, notable for its very contemporary use of geometric clipped foliage, and gardens by Tom Stuart-Smith. 'He also works with lines which link with the landscape – he is one of the designers whose work I follow the most enthusiastically,' he says. Finally he mentions le Jardin Plume in Normandy, for 'its combination of straight lines and

naturalistic planting'. What Machiel recognizes in most of these gardens is the contemporary take on one of the most successful tropes in garden design history – the creative tension between geometry and loose planting. Initially expressed in 20th-century England as a response to a love for Italian formality combined with an enthusiasm for the artless informality of cottage gardens, the style has evolved as contemporary exponents have tended to reduce and simplify the formal element and play up the planting.

'I like wide landscapes,' he says. 'I like the typical Dutch landscape: windmills, water, grasses, you don't get distracted.' He feels that the best designs he makes are the ones that bring the garden close to the surroundings, where he can draw lines out to connect the house to the wider landscape and make a link with it, which is not easy in the suburbs.

Machiel finds himself doing more and more coastal gardens. 'We are busy learning about coastal species and I like the colours in the dunes, the natural plant combinations.' *Hippophae rhamnoides* is a favourite, the sea buckthorn, a grey-leaved shrub with contrasting bright orange berries, and an incredible tolerance for dry

sandy soils – although with its suckering habit, it can be a challenging plant to use in the garden.

It is clear from a walk around the average Dutch suburb that many garden owners choose low maintenance above all else for the garden, buying conifers or ground cover, or if they want a minimal level of work, hydrangeas or plane trees (*Platanus × acerifolia*) that can be clipped – a very traditional method. Worse still is Machiel's observation that in new developments, 60 per cent of gardens have hard surfaces, artificial grass or decking with no plants. Fortunately, the problem that this poses for the environment, particularly concerning runoff during heavy rainfall or storms, is recognized; the local government of Den Haag is now giving grants for green roofs and paying property owners to remove paving so that rainwater can drain away naturally.

Designers like Machiel who love plants and want to extend the range of species used are inevitably frustrated by this modern trend. However, while many of Machiel's customers still say they want low maintenance, some are beginning to favour the plants that have become popular in recent years, with more grasses and a naturalistic effect. 'At school we did not learn anything about perennials and grasses, and we were taught to always cut everything down before winter, which I

04

Nepeta × faassenii forms a low sprawling mat of grey foliage, with a long season of lilac blue flowers; the visiting butterfly is a small tortoiseshell (*Aglais urticae*)

05

The foliage of santolina alongside a maritime *objet trouvé*.

06

Marco Márquez (left) and Machiel Vlieland.

used to do, but my vision has changed,' he says. 'Autumn and winter are the most important times as that's when you can see the garden at its clearest, but it can be tough making sure it looks good during that period.'

Machiel designs 40–50 gardens a year. On the whole, he feels that his gardens look best after three to four years when the owners begin to do things their own way, adding objects and plants that he himself would never have used, such as 'Buddha heads or ugly garden furniture'. Ideally, he says, he will negotiate some co-operation with the customer's gardener, but many only call once or twice a year, in which case he tries to persuade them to arrange more regular visits. Like many garden designers, he feels that some clients are very passive, preferring to sit in their gardens without becoming involved with any maintenance.

'The best customers are those who like to be in the garden and do some work there, not just treating it as another inanimate space,' says Machiel. Some clients do become inspired, and keep on returning for advice on maintenance or his opinion on their own decisions. There is indeed a general division between garden designers who essentially create outdoor rooms which are seen by their owners as relatively static and those who are more interested in working with plants and creating a natural environment. Clients who also take

an interest in the planting of the gardens they commission often develop ongoing relationships with designers, whose role then segues from designer to consultant.

In wanting to promote gardens that bring nature close to the home, Machiel is keen to use environmentally friendly materials, including those which do not involve many transport miles, which means ideally of Dutch origin, or from next-door Belgium or Germany at the most distant. Hard materials need to have the soft tones that enable them to blend harmoniously with the subtle colours of dune vegetation. The strongest is the rust colour of weathered corten steel, but he feels that this is a colour that relates to the dunes – too bright to be called brown, too dull to be orange, this powerful earth colour makes a statement in his gardens that is emphatic but never jarring. The contrast and creative tension between hard landscaping and the planting in gardens is something that particularly inspires and interests Machiel. He even finds himself fascinated by the Atlantic Wall, a wartime concrete construction that runs along part of the Dutch coastline and creates a dramatic contrast with the soft and highly mobile sandy landscape around it.

The colours of Machiel's coastal gardens perfectly reflect those of the dune vegetation: greys, dull or dark greens, pale straw tones. Grasses play a

huge role, for those now commercially available are nearly all reliably long-lived (the ever-popular and tactile *Stipa tenuissima* being the main exception, although often vigorously self-seeding). They are supremely suitable for coastal gardens as the strength of their stems is combined with a suppleness that makes them windproof. Over the longer term, the creeping mat of growth and accompanying dense root network hold loose sandy soils together. Accompanying the grasses are low-growing shrubby species, some of which are north European in origin, such as the sea buckthorn or small willows, but many Mediterranean species are used as well. This may seem a paradox to some, but the growing season for these plants – lavenders, *Santolina chamaecyparissus*, species of *Nepeta* – is the cooler months and this coastline is windy rather than cold; these are plants that survive wind well.

Coastal gardens may seem niche, but the plants that flourish in them are ideal for many testing urban environments, given their tolerance of drought, salt and exposure. Machiel may be onto a good thing in making them central to his design ethic.

INSPIRED BY NATURAL LANDSCAPES

01
Corten steel cuts through
Calamagrostis × acutiflora
'Karl Foerster', a very
windproof grass.

02
Lavandula angustifolia
and yellow great mullein
(*Verbascum olympicum*)
in one of Machiel's
coastal gardens.

03/04
Ammophila arenaria, the
marram grass that holds
sand dunes together.

05
Young plants of
Calamagrostis × acutiflora
'Karl Foerster'.

06
Pinus pinaster, a notably
wind-tolerant pine.

03

04

05

06

 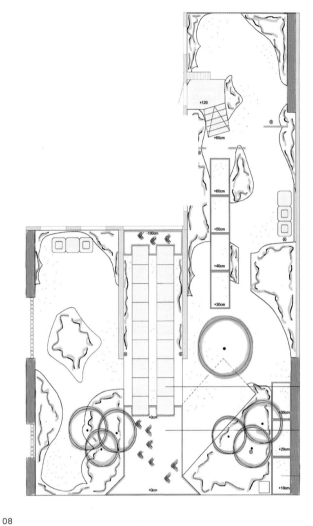

07

08

09

07
An evergreen hedge of oleaster (*Elaeagnus ebbingei*).

08
This plan of one of Machiel's gardens shows great contrasts of soft and strong forms.

09
The slightly bowed corten steel sheets indisputably interrupt the 'streaming' path, but correspond very well with the nearby plants in their natural tone.

10
Eryngium planum, closely related to *E. maritimum*, but an easier plant for average garden conditions.

11
Santolina forms a compact low shrub and is more amenable to pruning than many similar Mediterranean plants.

10

11

SANDY
HEATHLAND

The sky over the Dutch heathlands is big, and it feels even bigger than the normal expanse of Dutch sky – possibly because this land is one we don't expect to be as perfectly level as it actually is. It is uncultivated, and we are used to flat landscapes with big skies being green with rye grass, occasionally dotted by cows, crossed at least once within our field of sight by a canal or ditch, perhaps a dyke to slightly intrude on the perfect hemisphere of the sky, and a building and some trees to stab its perfection too. There is none of that here, although there are some pine trees and a line of woodland to ruffle the horizon in at least one direction.

The predominant colour is the dull purple-brown of heather, its foliage darkened by a dry summer, some still in flower with the bright pink-purple that can turn this whole landscape into a vibrantly colourful place. There is some grass in the form of wispy pale yellow seedheads, some bracken, and quite a lot of bare soil, although bare sand might be a better description of it.

'Heathland', the name we give in English to this landscape, and which in Dutch is *heide*, can be found all over The Netherlands, but its greatest extent and strongest historical associations are with Brabant, where it sweeps over the imperceptible border with Belgium. Heathland, or heath, is a type of vegetation and habitat which is unique to northern Europe, especially Germany,

Denmark, Belgium, The Netherlands and the UK; it can be found in other European countries, but on a much smaller scale. There is a great similarity here with the moors of Scotland and northern England, except that these are hilly and rocky and exposed to the elements by altitude, not dead flat and just above sea level.

Heath/*heide* come from an Old Germanic word that covers both 'wasteland' and the plants that grow on it. And wasteland is how previous generations thought of it; our ancestors would have found our now rather positive view of heathland very strange. For us it is big open space, and the fact that there is no sign of habitation, or roads or farming, is something positive, especially when the wind drops, and there is that rare commodity in the modern world – *silence*.

At a time when most of us are inhabitants of cities and are surrounded for most of our lives by the physical reality of our civilization, these big, open, unimproved, unmanaged, wild, sometimes frightening spaces feel very precious indeed. They are places to walk, to ride or cycle, places in which to decompress and feel close to the natural world. Websites, tourist leaflets and guidebooks all stress how this is a landscape of recreation, of wilderness, of total contrast to the stressed normality of our busy lives.

Visit heathland, especially one of the bigger expanses of Brabant, in anything other than perfect weather and you will see another side to it. Indeed one of the pleasures of exploring these places as a tourist is that slight air of menace, the awareness that once the wind gets up and the rain starts falling these are very unpleasant places to be, especially if you have lost your bearings (easily done) and cannot remember which one of the several almost identical car parks you have left your vehicle in. Now is the time to cast your mind back to our predecessors' days and imagine walking or riding across these spaces in a storm, when these heaths once covered vastly more land than they do today. Getting lost here could easily have been fatal.

To our predecessors, these heathlands were indeed landscapes of menace: exposed to the elements, difficult to navigate, and also useless. The only people who were able to gain anything

from them were very poor, grazing a few animals on the scrubby grass, collecting heather to make brooms or to tie into faggots and sell as firewood, or perhaps keeping bees for honey. All too often poverty and remoteness led to people becoming brigands; for much of history this was a factor that made crossing any of northern Europe's heathlands a nervewracking experience.

The heathlands' unsuitability for farming can be seen today from the sandy soil, which, once disturbed, can take a long time to grow a new crop of heather or grass. 'Ordinary' grass does not flourish, and it is such ordinary grass that is both the basis for animal husbandry and the sign that cereals can be grown – without either of these, any kind of productive agriculture is impossible. Not surprisingly heaths were seen, extremely negatively, as lands with no value and positively dangerous. A long struggle to convert them into more productive land gained speed in the late 19th century, fed by the hunger of increasing populations and technological innovation, and soon they were in headlong retreat.

While the Dutch struggle against the sea, with dykes, ditches and windmills, is known the world over, the other side of Dutch land- and country-making, the winning of the heaths, is much less well known, but arguably almost as important.

Until recently, when we began to value biodiversity and wilderness, and to realize the recreational importance of heathlands, the conquering of heaths was as much a part of the triumphalist narrative of Dutch national mission as was rolling back the sea.

The heaths feel wild and 'natural', but of course they are not at all natural. Very little is. We underestimate our remote ancestors and their ability to modify and manage nature. So fixated are we on modern environmental problems and their causes that we find it hard to believe our predecessors were also immensely destructive, and perhaps even more so as they did not understand the consequences of their actions.

All over northern and western Europe, people from the Stone Age onwards spread and multiplied. The climate, moderated by the sea (although it may not feel like this on a winter's day in Brabant) enables a long growing season, so the grass that feeds livestock has a good long run of staying green and photosynthesizing. Populations and their herds grew, in lockstep. Patchy forests covered much of Europe, the patches caused by the intense grazing of wild cattle and deer (and before that, mammoths, but sudden climate changes played an important role in their extinction). As the wild animals were hunted and gradually eliminated the herds took their place. As their numbers grew, the treeless patches expanded, the sheep, cattle and goats grazing their way through the

01
The Heath near Laren by the mid-19th-century painter Anton Mauve (1887).

02
Barn with Fence in Brabant by Willem Witsen (1892).

03
Heath Landscape by Willem Wenckebach (c.1893), featuring bog rosemary (*Andromeda polifolia*) and sundew (*Drosera* sp.).

02

03

thinning forests, preventing regeneration by eating tree saplings. On a fertile soil, grazing intensity had to be very high to prevent all regeneration, and anyway forests there had value as timber and plentiful firewood. The thin forests on poor sandy soils yielded little good timber and so had no value. Trees regenerated only slowly and so the herds gradually destroyed the forests, allowing heather and other tough plants tolerant of poor soils to take over.

A long process of deforestation meant that by the end of the Middle Ages the sandy soils of Dutch and Belgian Brabant had become largely treeless and barren. Most of the landscape was common land, with scattered villages where the dung from cattle and sheep penned overnight was laboriously collected and used as fertilizer on thin fields of wheat and rye. In some places the over-grazing was so bad that sand dunes began to form; in other places, they had already formed as a result of extensive logging to provide wood for furnaces used for the smelting of bog ore. The late 19th century saw both a need to increase the amount of agricultural land and the means by which to do so, and the heathlands came under a two-pronged attack. One was through forestry, with the foundation in 1899 of the Staatsbosbeheer, a state body for the promotion of forestry, particularly using pine, which grew well on the sandy soils. The other was the use of newly invented chemical fertilizers which at last enabled large areas of intrinsically low-fertility land to grow productive crops.

01

02

03

04

01
Elderly pines on the Strabrechtse Heide near Heeze, North Brabant.

02
Forest alternating with open heath is typical of the wilder areas of North Brabant.

03
Molinia caerulea, a classic grass of poor acidic soils, now much used in gardens.

04
Bodies of water are often the result of a history of peat-digging.

Turning heathland into good farmland took time, and before the development of tractors in the 20th century, the grubbing up of heather and tussock grasses had to be done by hand and horse. Attracting men to work in the sparsely populated areas became part of a national mission, and one with distinct political overtones. The Oranjebond van Orde (Orange Order) was set up in 1893 to attract young people from the cities to move to the heathlands, explicitly to undermine labour unrest and socialist political activism in urban areas, the name indicating that going to work

digging heather was also an act of loyalty to the house of Orange, that is, the royal family. There were other organizations too, such as the Kwartguldenvereniging (Quarter Guilder Union) a women's organization that supported the Orange Order. A bank created to help people buy homes and fund business was dissolved in 1922 after the director was found to be misusing funds.

The conservation movement started by Jac. P. Thijsse and others in the 1930s finally brought the 'reclamation' of the heathlands under control and the second half of the 20th century saw many of the

remaining areas given formal protection as nature reserves and national parks. Fortunately, some of the newly protected areas included areas of high biodiversity, such as De Groote Peel, which is of vital importance for migrating birds including the magnificent but now rare crane. Today, our perception of heathlands is very different to that of previous generations as we value their wildlife, appreciate their emptiness and use heathers and grasses as garden and landscape plants.

05

06

07

05
The burnet *Sanguisorba tenuifolia* var. *purpurea* is a garden plant very similar to the wild *S. officinalis* of the heathland.

06
Heather (*Calluna vulgaris*) is the dominant plant over large areas. It is the source of some of the finest honey.

07
Sandy soils limit plant diversity over wide areas, with heather and brooms dominant.

Frank van der Linden

Garden designer Frank van der Linden's taste in plants definitely tends towards the wilder end of the spectrum. This can be appreciated by a walk around his own, relatively new garden, laid out in 2016 at his home in Sterksel, near Eindhoven. It is relatively small, some 2500 sq m (3000 sq yd), partially shaded by the mature trees in his neighbour's garden, and is clearly the garden of a 'plant nut'. The planting is dense but not crowded, and very diverse. 'I like to plant a scheme and allow the plants to take over, letting them seed and go their own way,' he says. 'It is more personal and wilder than the gardens I often design and not everyone likes it – if I show it to potential clients it can sometimes put them off, and we don't hear from them again.'

All garden designers talk about how they listen to clients, but few follow this up with being very open about what they really think; Frank is a bit more forthright. 'It is good to listen to clients, but what they want is sometimes different to what they ask for, because often they do not know what they want.' Second-guessing people's real desires is an important part of the business.

'I'm fascinated by nature, and for me the wild flowers along the roadsides are one of the big inspirations,' says Frank. 'Around here we also have the Brabant heathland, which is an inspiration and a guideline for understanding nature. So this area is in my blood. I think that my passion for native plants started here. As a kid I used to go out by myself into the immense fields of heather and woods. I collected saplings to plant in my parents' garden. Some plants, such *Myrica gale*, are on the 'red list' and so are protected. When I was 11 years old, it was almost like an addiction to go out and collect plants and for this myrica I once went out alone on a dark evening into the heather to collect a few shoots with roots. I was excited to plant them in my self-made swamp at home!'

Frank's design company is named Van Nature, because, he says, 'What I am doing is my nature, and I have been doing it as long as I can remember. I started straight after school – I chose a four-year training, but I am also self-taught, for learning is a continuous process.' He is firm that his family are definitely not gardeners. 'They were farmers, and had been so for generations, although my grandmother had the same plant tic – I remember she gave me some clivias, so I am the third generation to have them.' In fact, Frank's grandfather was one of the pioneers in Brabant during the great era of land reclamation; in the 1920s he cleared land for a local lord and was rewarded with rent-free status on his own land for five years.

Frank started his garden design company in 2000 and ran it for seven years. 'I had four or five employees – we did anything the client wanted us to do, but then I wanted to change,' he says. He took a trip to Mont Ventoux in Provence in his old Citroën 2CV to think about his life, and walking the bare limestone with its unique garrigue vegetation helped him reconsider his priorities.

'I felt a passion for a more naturalistic style of gardening. I just wanted to use my knowledge to give advice to my clients, and to work more with the plants, so I changed the way I operated. I began to grow the plants myself, as I increasingly wanted to use plants in clients' gardens which I could not find in nurseries.'

So for a number of years Frank did just that, making gardens with plants he grew himself, which is of course what Piet and Anja Oudolf had done. However, the Dutch nursery trade has since changed, with plant availability, especially of perennials, soaring. Such self-sufficiency is no longer necessary and in 2018 Frank closed the nursery.

'I remember the Priona Garden – it made such a big impression,' he says. 'I first went when Henk Gerritsen was alive, 15 or so years ago. I loved the balance of nature and horticulture. That's what makes it a form of art.' Frank describes himself as being a huge Mien Ruys fan, 'Although when I was younger I did not appreciate the style of the period, it just looked dated and her paving and railway sleepers were everywhere. Mien was very good at planting design, but everyone copied her and the people who did that were usually excellent builders, but with no knowledge of planting design.' His feelings about Piet Oudolf are more straightforward; he describes him as 'a huge inspiration for me'.

Frank's own garden is certainly very naturalistic, but there is the solidity of defined structure that is such a defining characteristic of even the wildest Dutch garden.

Here this structure takes the form of several mounds of clipped evergreen foliage with a small tree emerging from the top, a combination that has become something of a signature. The clipped mounds here are privet, *Ligularia vulgaris*, with emerging *Amelanchier* or *Sorbus aucuparia*, but he has also used beech *(Fagus)*, *Ilex meservae*, *Elaeagnus ebbingei* and *Salix rosmarinifolia*, often with *Prunus subhirtella* emerging.

The planting is in layers, a technique Frank regards as central to making the most of diversity and maximizing seasonal spread. Beginning in March, primroses *(Primula vulgaris)* spread yellow over most of the garden, as they seed here vigorously alongside species bulbs. Later on, low to medium-height shade-tolerant perennials take over: species of *Geranium*, *Pulmonaria* and *Epimedium* along with *Viola odorata*, and then taller summer-flowering perennials and grasses. Such layering sounds, and is, logical, but in reality it requires considerable skill in plant placement and spacing. Plants that die down in summer, such as bulbs, are easy; those that become semi-dormant and tolerate some shade, for example primulas, can be shoehorned in among taller perennials; but those that must have more light, such as epimediums, cannot be. There are a lot of variations on this layering theme: violas forming dense ground cover beneath the expansive leaves of *Darmera peltata*, the elegant lush green foliage of the grass *Hakonechloa macra* spreading among the grey leaves of bearded iris, and the distinctively marked leaves of *Geranium phaeum* varieties popping up between other plants, often having seeded themselves in.

01
Autumn moor grass
(Sesleria autumnalis)
makes a great filler,
highlighting the forms and
colours of the perennials
around it.

01

01
Calamagrostis × acutiflora 'Karl Foerster' is a first-rate grass for long seasonal interest.

02
Grasses highlight perennial seedheads.

03
Mexican feather grass (*Stipa tenuissima*) seedheads last well into the winter.

01

02

03

Grasses play a big role in all Frank's gardens. 'No grasses, no garden, I think,' he says. 'I need them for structure between flowering plants in summer and for colour in the autumn and winter.'

Sometimes he masses them, for example with *Stipa tenuissima*, the extremely feathery seedheads of which create a small-scale stylized meadow effect, or using big groups of *Carex muskingumensis*, a semi-evergreen sedge whose habit of clumps of stems with leaves running all the way up is quite unlike any other, and creates an almost hedge-like effect when massed. He will also plant several different grass species together to show off the contrasts

between them, something few other designers do, and indeed almost seem to have an aversion to doing.

The high proportion of grasses used emphasizes the naturalistic quality of Frank's designs, but nevertheless in most of the gardens he has designed there are clipped woody plants too – box, beech and hawthorn. At his former home, he even had some very Mien Ruys-inspired low box blocks which marched across a paved area before plunging into a perennial border. 'Naturalistic' in other garden cultures often eschews such 'formal' inclusions, but not here, and the resulting creative tension can be very effective.

Frank is very conscious that working with plants is a long-term learning process.

'It takes years to get to know how plants behave in different conditions,' he says, 'particularly now that I am trying to make more natural combinations where plants can spread and do their own thing.'

Continuity through the year is something he sees as being particularly important, and the layered approach to planting makes this a lot easier to plan, to implement and to manage. The planting in his own garden points to a love of diversity, with a high number of species per square metre, which is perhaps why he expresses caution about plants that spread vigorously, which others might welcome as a rapidly forming graphic block; *Pycnanthemum pilosum* is

04
Narrow paths through perennials encourage us to observe them closely.

05
Box cut into neat cubes contrasts well with perennials.

06
Several cultivars of eulalia grass (*Miscanthus sinensis*).

05

04   06

one example of a plant he does not wish to use again, though another designer might welcome it for its ability to form extensive patches.

Planting design is clearly a very intuitive and emotional business for Frank. 'Really, sometimes I can't sleep because of all the ideas in my head,' he says. 'It's a real joy! I get energy from it, just as I did when I was a kid.

I like to set out the plants in any garden alone, in peace and quiet. It's my special moment, and I won't let my employee help me because I will lose my concentration and flow.'

Many of Frank's gardens are rural, large in scale and beneath big skies, where grasses and large perennials are a perfect fit. One of his smaller gardens, though, was created for a floral artist who runs a small commercial picking garden, 'I liked his planting style, as he has a very intuitive relationship with plants,' she says. Her own town garden in Helmond uses raised corten steel planters with colourful flowers for cutting, while the rest of the garden, partly shaded by a huge tulip tree, is wilder, with grasses, perennials and clipped beech mounds, ending in a wonderful two-storey wooden children's playhouse and a work area behind a screen.

'I'm on my own path,' says Frank, 'designing more and more with the plants that are native to the area where I live.'

He aims to integrate them with the cultivated flora he uses so proficiently, partly to help improve the content of his gardens for biodiversity in the form of specialist insect species. The balance between the cultivated and the wild he achieves is a delicate one which looks set to continually and gloriously evolve.

01

02

03

01
The classic Citroën HY van
that Frank once used for
plant fairs.

02
The anise hyssop
Agastache 'Blue Fortune'
has attractive seedheads.

03
Frank has grown his own
plants for his design
work too.

04
Blocks of the sedge Carex
muskingumensis.

05
Yellow Rudbeckia
tomentosa 'Henry Eilers'
and Anemone × hybrida
'Serenade'.

04

06
Dense borders give an immersive feel.

07
The reflexed petals of purple coneflower (*Echinacea pallida*).

08
The flowers of great burnet (*Sanguisorba officinalis*).

09
Black fountain grass (*Pennisetum alopecuroides* 'Moudry'); backlighting is often best for grasses.

10
Echinacea purpurea 'Magnus'; the seedheads of this coneflower will carry on looking good after the flowers are gone.

05

06

07

08

09

10

01
Ostrich fern
(*Matteuccia
struthiopteris*).

02
The border as spring
turns to summer.

03
One of Frank's
garden plans.

04
Pastel shades are
at their best in very
early summer.

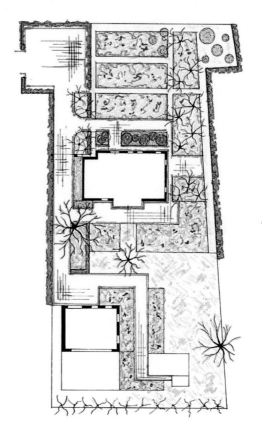

01

02

03

04

05

06

07

05
Calamagrostis brachytricha. Grasses are often great performers as everything else declines.

06
Native hemp agrimony (*Eupatorium cannabinum*) can be seen in the foreground.

07
Miscanthus grasses add bulk to a planting.

08
Box plants clipped into oval shapes.

08

01

02

01
Lesser quaking grass
(*Briza minor*) mixes well
with perennials.

02
A border in very light
shade.

03
Angelica archangelica,
a magnificent biennial.

04
Gardens are always
social spaces.

05
A corten steel raised bed.

03

04

05

INSPIRED BY NATURAL LANDSCAPES

06

07

08

09

10

06
*Objets trouvés have
year-round interest.*

07
The axis of an urban
garden.

08
A children's playhouse
and wood store.

09
A place to entertain.

10
Potentilla nepalensis
'Miss Willmott'.

11
The area of transition
from sun to shade can be
a pleasant place to sit in
the garden.

12
Briza minor with
Echinacea pallida.

11

ROCKS & HILLS

South Limburg is different to the rest of The Netherlands, but not to the rest of northern Europe. Anyone from outside the country will find the rolling hills with their fields, patches of woodland, occasional hedges and farmhouses nestled in shallow valleys quite unexceptional. Compared to the rest of the country, however, its slopes and folds make it very different; everyone else's normal is here exceptional. The iconography of everyday life is firmly Dutch – the houses, the road signs, the advertizing, the shop-fronts – and yet this sits uneasily on the unfamiliarity, or at least the un-Dutchness of the landscape.

The highest hill in the country is here, the Vaalserberg – at 322 m (1056 ft) nothing very dramatic, but significant in a country where a large part of the land is below sea level. Much of the landscape is made up of plateaux, the result of many millennia of erosion levelling the land to gentle hills, but then cut into by the river Meuse, creating terraces, although to see these does require some trust in the vision of a geologist to lead us to read the landscape.

And then there is rock. Not much to see, only the occasional outcrop, but little knowledge of geology is required to realize that there is plenty of it below those hills – the visible landscape is a thin layer of soil and vegetation over that rock, whereas in much of the rest of the country there is no rock until you hit it with a drilling rig, many metres down. Much of the province is underlaid with marl, a soft limestone

with a high clay content. Some areas are covered in loess, the very soft rock that resulted from the consolidation of vast amounts of dust being blown onto the land after the last Ice Age. Loess provides fertile soils, and is not surprisingly easily eroded or dug into.

Most romantic here are the holloways, where the erosive power of water has been combined with that of thousands of pairs of feet and horses' hooves over many centuries, wearing down the paths so that they have gradually sunk into the soft rock, forming a gully.

Holloways are particularly likely to form in rocks that, however soft, have good vertical holding qualities, such as both marl and loess. The origins of the holloways are

often very old, and their presence in the landscape is a powerful reminder of the antiquity of the human presence here. This in itself is another distinction from the rest of the country, where so much is relatively new, or has been reorganized so many times that we have no idea of its history. A holloway is something that speaks to us very directly of the ways in which people have needed to travel, and that act of travelling has worn its way metres into the ground.

The form of the natural and cultural landscape does not differ much between the three countries that form the greater region. Universal north European features of geological process and cultural landscape shaping are in evidence: rivers sculpt landforms, farmers demarcate their land, and lords build castles. Particularly notable are the Lichtenberg Castle ruins on the Sint

Pietersberg, a remnant of one of the rare high castles in the Northern Netherlands; the mount, at the northern end of a plateau of soft limestone, is another radically unusual place for the country. Always a valuable commodity for building, limestone has a special value here. Marl or limestone would also have been burnt for making lime, vital for making mortar for building, or, from the 19th century onwards, for scattering on the fields to boost fertility. There are 'marl caves' where quarrying has taken the search for quality stone deep into the hills, and indeed the hill here is honeycombed with a network of caves – the surviving 60 km (40 miles) or so are even a tourist attraction. Nearby there are still a few cave houses. Limestone, as any botanist will tell you, produces a particularly rich array of wild flowers, despite supporting only thin and dry soils, and the plateau is the only place in The Netherlands with this rather special habitat. The pale yellow limestone sometimes penetrates the soil, particularly on banks, making for striking contrasts with the green grass. This calcareous flora is one which those who make wild flower meadows are always keen to exploit, and indeed many of its elements, such as lady's bedstraw *(Galium verum)* and knapweed *(Centaurea scabiosa)* are regarded as crucial to a successfully biodiverse garden meadow.

There is an odd irony here. The colourful wild flowers of limestone grassland are naturally limited to these specialized habitats and locations. Urban civilization, however, loves limestone, turning it into concrete, then demolishing whatever it was built into and crushing and refashioning it into more concrete.

Urban environments then become increasingly like these precious habitats, and given that the early 21st century has also seen an enormous growth in the use of wild flower seed mixes along roadsides, the results are the onward march of this colourful and biodiverse flora as it takes to the shallow concrete- and rubble-polluted soils of urban areas with joyful alacrity.

    Ways of managing land, growing crops, keeping animals – all are very international, for the demands of the land, the climate and economics determine them. Whereas in most Dutch landscapes it is the need to manage water that takes priority, in South Limburg the human need to manage agriculture can come first.

01

03

05

02

04

06

07

08

10

09

11   12

The form that it takes is dictated by what the land can offer, which because of the somewhat hilly terrain means a patchwork of fields of varying sizes, small patches of woodland, and hedgerows. Technically, this is a *bocage* landscape, 'bocage' being a word derived from the Latin for wood, meaning one where woody plants – trees, hedges and small woods – are widely scattered and integrated into the landscape, playing a definite visual and economic role.

The relationship of the viewer, which these days increasingly means the walker or cyclist, with a hilly bocage landscape is a very different one to that with a flat landscape and even more to a polder one. In much of the flat Dutch landscape, the viewer is immersed so that they cannot see very far. Any elevation, such as the few metres of a dyke, immediately grants the privilege of seeing further, usually through 360 degrees, a bit like suddenly being able to see a living map; in fact that privilege is often a necessity, as those who are not used to reading the subtleties of these landscapes can all too easily get lost. Limburg, though, does not offer the prospect of the instant bird's-eye view but instead the gradual unravelling that any hilly landscape offers, the rounding of the bend, the topping of a rise giving a new perspective. The journey becomes more like the unrolling of a Chinese scroll, as one scene follows another. It is a very different perspective.

01
Holloways can magically route us through the countryside.

02
A warm slope can support a vineyard.

03
Field poppy (*Papaver rhoeas*) and corn marigold (*Glebionis segetum*) at a field edge.

04
The caves left behind after mining for marl have even temperatures that make them ideal for storage.

05
Brown knapweed (*Centaurea jacea*), a common wild flower of dry fields and woodland edges.

06
Caves at Maastricht left by mining for marl, once used in farming.

07
A limestone quarry for cement manufacture.

08
Loess makes for lushly fertile well-drained land, ideal for arable crops.

09
Vineyards are increasingly a feature of the area.

10
Marl is a sedimentary rock, long ago deposited out of lime in a shallow sea.

11
Field poppies (*Papaver rhoeas*) along a broad field boundary.

12
A typical farm track of the region, with a recently pollarded willow.

Noël van Mierlo

It is intriguing that, early in conversation, Noël van Mierlo starts to talk about someone else. Intriguing, as Noël comes across very much as a perfectionist, a craftsman who pays enormous attention to every detail and does not commit to anything unless he can do it really well. Perfectionists often have a problem with delegation, but clearly not Noël. 'I want to be able to make a good product,' he says, 'and that can mean collaboration.' The someone else Noël was so keen to talk about was the botanist and plant specialist Ruurd van Donkelaar, whom he employs as a planting design consultant. He is clearly the most important of several such specialists. 'Working with them makes sense, as each one of us can only know so much,' says Noël. 'I consider myself a director. I write a script, I look after composition and spatial relations, then, if needed, I search for collaborators who can make it work. When I was younger, and working as part of my parents' ambitious landscape company, I was surrounded by specialists, a lot of them older and wiser then I was. So, collaborating to get the job done really comes naturally to me.'

Who then is Ruurd van Donkelaar, of whom Noël speaks so warmly? He is essentially a planting design consultant, a botanist and grower, from a family which has been involved with plants for several generations. 'I saw him give a lecture at least 12 years ago, and I asked if we could work together as I thought we would fit well,' says Noël. Since then, he has involved Ruurd in his projects on many occasions. Noël designs the garden plan with the routes and the basic spatial layout, and handpicks the first layer of trees and shrubs as part of the architecture, but discusses them with Ruurd. The lower, perennial layer is then very often left to Ruurd.

There is a certain humility here, a case of knowing one's limits. Landscape architects, and garden designers even more so, generally expect to do the planting and are certainly expected to do so by the public, but specialist knowledge recognized and bought in inevitably leads to better results.

'To be really good with plants you have to be obsessed. Ruurd (pictured right) understands deeply how nature works,' says Noël. 'Crucially, having his knowledge in my pocket makes me free, and it gives me confidence to work with gardens on every soil.'

Noël's gardens are perhaps the least Dutch of those in this book. With their naturalistic water bodies, absence of straight lines, combination of organic form and bold design, and above all their use of rock, they belong to a particular globally popular genre with an ancestry perhaps best summed up by the Chinese concept of mountain-and-water which is at the core of the Asian tradition, but which has, over a long period, seeped into the Western consciousness too. They are reminiscent of early 20th-century rock and water gardens or the so-called Pacific North West style of that region of the United States. 'A lot of my clients have lived or travelled abroad, often in the US or the Far East,' Noël says. 'They recognize their life abroad in my work.'

Rock is that most alien of materials in Holland. 'I work with it because nobody else does here and I love the material,' he says. 'Rock is somewhere between hard and soft landscaping, a perfect tool to blend with different elements, and they give a garden age and weight.' In many ways Noël's work is not particularly Dutch, but reflects instead the experiences and appreciations of someone who has travelled. 'I am inspired by architects in places like the western United States or Norway,' he says. 'One step and they have to fit into nature. They dance with nature but find a place for the architecture to flourish. I love that.'

Of course, these are two places where there is a lot of rock and they are far removed from the lush Dutch lowlands. Nevertheless, people travel, and inevitably travel shapes their experiences and, for those in the creative professions, their sense of what is aesthetically pleasing and what they want to create. Noël spent a year living in Canada, and describes how he misses its vast forests which are not to be found in The Netherlands.

01
The interweaving of water, land, water plants and trees, with a pavilion as the focal point, evokes East Asian gardens, and the harmonious balancing of elements central to that tradition.

01

01

02

03

04

INSPIRED BY NATURAL LANDSCAPES

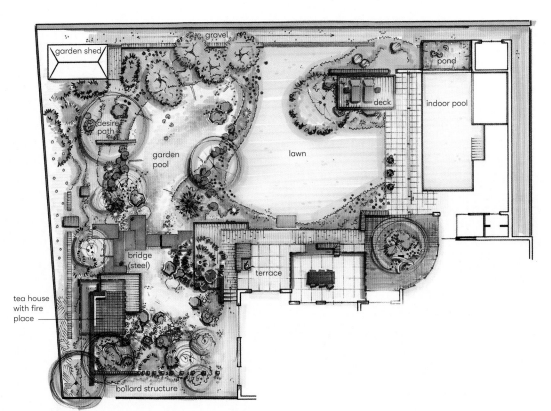

Labels within plan:

garden shed

gravel

pond

deck

indoor pool

desire path

garden pool

lawn

bridge (steel)

terrace

tea house with fire place

bollard structure

01
A garden pool with gravel edges that make it look truly natural.

02
A tussock of the grass *Hakenochloa macra*.

03
A branch of tupelo (*Nyssa sylvatica*) in autumn colour.

04
Ginkgo biloba turned butter yellow in autumn.

05
This plan of the garden clearly shows the structure.

06
Rectilinear geometries make an effective contrast to the naturalistic planting.

05

06

01

INSPIRED BY NATURAL LANDSCAPES

Noël's garden design work is in many ways very global, and that is perhaps itself very Dutch; this is a country and culture that has nearly always looked outwards, enthused by and borrowing from all that the world has to offer. Clients, too, often want their gardens to remind them of more dramatic environments than their homeland; Noël has one who likes walking in the Alps, and wanted him to bring something of the feeling of the mountains into the garden. The rocks he uses are sourced in the Belgian Ardennes. They appear in his gardens in a way that is remarkably natural, not just fine-looking specimens but accompanying smaller pieces and the finer particles which they break down naturally into, so the overall effect is that of a garden built on this material as its bedrock. Ground cover and other smaller plants weave in and out of the stone. Ruurd's influence is what ensures the presence of these low-growing plants, a level of detail a great many garden designers all too often rather ignore.

Noël's father ran a garden design and build company. 'My childhood garden was an experience of living in a designed garden,' he recalls. As he grew up he started working as a landscaper at different companies, then joined his parents' company and took it over in 2005. 'I was the son of the boss, which makes you alone,' he says, 'but leading a team of experienced landscapers was an important experience. My father's work was all about craftsmanship and he loved the building aspect of our trade. I like to think that my gardens are a celebration of craftsmanship too. The structures I build are "naked" in that I want people to see how they are built, and to show honest craftsmanship.' At this time he entered numerous competitions as he believed that most landscape companies in the country were tending to work in the same way, and he felt that competitions were a means of showing people a different approach.

01
Bronze-purple *Ajuga
reptans* 'Atropurpurea'
and grey-leaved *Nepeta
racemosa* 'Superba'.

01
Luzula sylvatica
with *Ajuga reptans*
'Atropurpurea'.

02
Trees break the line of
the boundary and so
help make the garden
feel limitless.

03
Blue-flowered
*Ceratostigma
plumbaginoides*.

04
Carex morrowii
'Gilt Edge'.

01

02

03

04

INSPIRED BY NATURAL LANDSCAPES

05
Traditional pavers allow for creative feathered edgings.

06
Strong lines contrast with naturalistic planting.

07
Rough paths gather moss at the edges.

08
Nepeta racemosa 'Superba'.

09
Hart's-tongue fern (*Phyllitis scolopendrium*).

In early 2012, following the economic crisis of the years before, Noël had to go out of business. 'It was the worst nightmare, having to close down and lay people off,' he says. Some hard and deep rethinking followed, and he decided to become a designer rather than a contractor. So, later that year, he started up a design office. In the second year of the new business, Noël was asked to design a garden where there was a leak in the pond – and as so often seems to happen in the garden business, one thing led to another. He and the client discussed the design of the garden, and the latter said he liked the Eastern look because of his extensive travels in Asia. Sensing a great opportunity, Noël decided to make a proposal and draw the best garden he could imagine. This commission turned out to be an ideal breakthrough, with a client who enabled him to reinvent himself and show what he could do. He filmed and documented everything over the two and a half years it took to create the garden; the main part was finished in 2015, and in 2018 he started on the ambitious front garden.

That garden has become known as 'The Japanese Water Garden', which is perhaps somewhat unfortunate as so many gardens in the West with this appellation are little more than clichés, and there is a question mark over whether it is really possible to make an authentic Japanese garden outside Japan. Noël says, 'If you avoid the clichés of a Japanese garden you are left with an adventure, the chance of doing something different but with a strong sense of harmony. There is a Japanese aesthetic at the core of the garden combined with a sense of the Western world's modernity.' Harmony is expressed by balance, with everything equally important. Entered for the British Society of Garden Designers awards in 2019, the garden won Best International Garden and the People's Choice Award.

01

01
The spacings of the wooden post barrier slowly change, altering our perspective.

02
Rocks provide escape routes and perches for amphibians.

03
A clump of *Pontederia cordata* expands slowly into the water.

02

03

Noël began doing water gardens a long time ago. For him, water acts as a focus for his aim to 'create a place where you can experience nature and the seasons, the different types of light, different plants – the pond, the boardwalk, these are all magnets that lure you into the garden and tempt you to explore it'.

This is perhaps the key to his gardens – exploring them is more like unrolling an Oriental scroll painting than walking across or through a plan. Water bodies that dominate gardens force you to walk around them, so the exploration-journey becomes something which has a beginning and an end, again like a scroll.

Another success for him is blurring boundaries so that it is not possible to discern where the garden ends, and a tree which is actually three or four gardens distant becomes part of the view. The occasional spontaneous appearance of interesting and attractive wild flora in his gardens is also a kind of blurring of culture and nature as well as being complementary to his planting. To successfully blend the experience of the garden with that of the surrounding world is a kind of subtle triumph for Noël's modest approach to crafting space.

01

01
Straight lines set up a creative tension with natural irregularities.

02
Native grass *Deschampsia cespitosa*; this is cultivar 'Bronzeschleier'.

03
The seedheads of *Heuchera micrantha*.

04
Acaena microphylla 'Kupferteppich', a low ground-cover plant.

05
The even lower *Leptinella squalida*.

02

03

04

05

06

07

08

09

06
The design of the boardwalks adds a subtle Japanese touch.

07
Taxus baccata makes a useful negative space.

08
Marginal plants such as *Pontederia cordata* blur pond boundaries.

09
Rock and irregular stone brings a touch of the wild to a suburban location.

MEADOWS
&
WOODLAND

The wild flowers stretch off in all directions, the yellow, white and purple-pink flowers at incredible densities, but in constantly changing proportions. What might perhaps surprise is that this is not a natural habitat, but one created artificially, a wild flower meadow that was sown as part of the landscaping of some new university buildings a few years previously.

That is one face of the Dutch meadow. Another is rather more common. In it, usually in June, it is not the wild flowers that we see, but the tractors mowing the uniform green sward. To many of us, used to thinking of agricultural machinery as rather slow and lumbering, they move incredibly fast. The cut grass lies in neat rows, later to be gathered up and sent off for silage making, again at great speed.

These are two extremes of the Dutch meadow, both completely artificial. 'Real' meadows can still be seen, but only rarely, in out-of-the-way corners in less heavily managed parts of the countryside, especially on old estates, or in nature reserves. These have a complex of grass and herb species of which the composition varies from place to place, depending on soil moisture content, chemistry and history. Often they are quite marginal places, so there will be areas dominated by more competitive grasses, or rushes, or even scrub and young trees. The uniformity of the agricultural meadow, or even the artificial wild flower meadow, is lacking.

'Meadow' can be a misunderstood word, now even more so, since their creation as landscape and garden features has resulted in a boom in popularity for them. The word is often used to describe any grass-dominated, reasonably flat and clearly delineated (usually by ditches) piece of countryside. In fact there is a very precise meaning, which tells us a lot. A meadow is vegetation which is mown every year as an agricultural crop, traditionally for hay (dry grass, to be stored to feed animals over the winter), more recently for silage (grass which is fermented, again to feed animals). A meadow is thus not at all natural, but a hybrid of natural ingredients, managed by humanity. Meadows have developed in Europe over many hundreds of years, as generations of farmers have made their annual cut. The particular combination of species is one which can survive, indeed thrive, under this cutting regime.

Meadow is distinct from pasture, which is vegetation cropped by livestock without being artificially cut; it too has its own distinct flora, but one which is less diverse, and less visually attractive. The modern meadow, however, is usually a monoculture of ryegrass. Scientifically led commercial agriculture favours silage production over hay – it is more nutritious, more efficient, and, crucially, is preferred by the customers, that is, cows. However, it is cut at least a month earlier than hay, which means that most of the wild flowers do not get a chance to flower and seed, and there are not many of them anyway in meadows managed for silage, as the fields are nearly all sown with ryegrass. This is a highly productive crop, a competitive grower, makes nutritious feed, and can be grown for years on the same ground, so long as it receives regular doses of high nitrogen and high phosphorus feed, and there is plenty of that around in terms of manure from all the cows. The reason for modern

01

02

03

04

05

06

pastureland being dominated by ryegrass is that it is very good for feeding dairy cows, which have been one of the main drivers of Dutch agricultural success. From the late medieval period onwards, as the peaty soils were drained to extract the peat, it was dairying that increasingly made sense.

Soils derived from peat are too poor for a good crop of wheat, or even the less demanding rye, in addition to which they were often wet, and became wetter as the soil continued to shrink. Some areas even became lakes, especially in the area north of Amsterdam. The drained but still soggy land did grow grass well enough, though, so the Dutch concentrated on producing milk, and turning it into butter and cheese for export. They did very well out of this, especially as Europe's populations expanded; everything began to revolve around the cow, and the life of the cow revolves inevitably around grass.

Dairy production has tended to dominate agriculture here ever since, so ryegrass makes complete sense in terms of agricultural productivity, but it eliminates other species. Ecologists refer to 'ryegrass deserts', arguing that there is considerably more biodiversity in the average stretch of desert than a Dutch field. They are of course right, but agriculture in The Netherlands is incredibly efficient; this country is, after all, the second biggest exporter of food in the world. However, ecologists and others concerned with nature question whether the almost obsessive reaching after ever-greater levels of efficiency and productivity should really be the national mission. There are those who look at the fields of silage rye grass, unmistakeable with their distinctive glossy leaves in summer sunshine, and see only the destruction of the diverse, colourful and insect-rich hay meadows of the past.

Much ryegrass has been sown after the ploughing up of the previously existing grassland, but just the application of manure slurry or chemical fertilizer can rapidly destroy the flora of an old hay meadow. Nitrogen and phosphorus preferentially favour the plants with the metabolism to gobble them up and make use of them. One application sees the stronger grasses begin to outcompete and suppress less vigorous ones and the herb element. Further applications see an almost complete grass takeover.

During the 1970s and 1980s, however, some ecologists and seed merchants started to develop meadow seed mixtures – combinations of the less vigorous grasses and the wild flowers typical of hay meadows. These were promoted to gardeners and landscape professionals as an alternative to mown grass, at the time a radical step, but one for which there had been much preparation, given the campaigning started by Jac. Thijsse in the early 1900s. Those who protested against the seemingly endless engineering of the countryside naturally supported this innovative use of a native plant community, both as an aesthetic element in private and community gardens, and a functional one along roadsides and in settings where corporate mown grass would have been the previous preferred option.

Among the companies which now sell wild flower meadow mixes is Cruydt-Hoeck, established by Rob Leopold and Dick van der Burg in 1978, initially to sell the seed of old-fashioned garden annuals as well as wild flowers. They developed the idea of the hardy annual mix for gardens which by the end of the century had become a well-established concept after it got taken up by bigger seed companies and by Nigel Dunnett at the University of Sheffield in northern England, who developed and promoted the concept as a cheap way for municipalities and landscape contractors to create amazingly colourful, pollinator-friendly temporary ornamental meadows. These have not been particularly important in The Netherlands, but Cruydt-Hoeck, under new management after the the death of its founders, has become a major supplier of native wild flower seed mixes which have enabled many large-scale wild flower habitat creation projects to take place up and down the country.

Summer now in The Netherlands is a much more flowery time than ever it used to be, with many roadsides spattered with colour. Much of the flora has not necessarily been sown; its presence is more about a change in management such as reduced mowing than any positive effort, the frequent presence of 'weed' species such as trefoil (*Lotus corniculatus*) and ribwort (*Plantago*) illustrating this. Among the best new habitats are those developments where nutrient-poor drier soil is matched with wild flowers which naturally thrive in such an environment. In nature, these are characteristic of thin limestone soils, found in a few places in Limburg, but building and landscape engineering works can leave behind soils which are ideal for this flora – in fact, the most diverse flora across northern Europe is that of shallow calcareous soils, ideal for the green spaces around new housing estates

07

08

09

01
Bird's-foot trefoil (*Lotus corniculatus*), flourishing in an area of grass cut once a year.

02
The borderland between land and water can be a valuable micro-habitat.

03
Common chicory (*Cichorium intybus*), parsnip (*Pastinaca sativa*), large teasel (*Dipsacus fullonum*), German chamomile (*Matricaria recutita*), bird's-foot trefoil (*Lotus corniculatus*), crimson clover (*Trifolium incarnatum*) and two species of sorrel (*Rumex* spp.)

04
A field of flax, which could be grown for fibre or as a source of linseed or linseed oil.

05
Jan Adriaenszoon Leeghwater (1575–1650), the engineer responsible for draining many of the lakes in the province of North Holland.

06
Water, grass, cows – the triumvirate which dominates so much of the Dutch countryside.

07
A map of 1573 showing the lakes north of Amsterdam, most of which are now either ryegrass fields or residential areas.

08
Landscape with Fishermen and Farmers Extracting Peat in a Marsh by Hendrik Willem Schweickhardt (1783).

09
Turf Stacking by Claes Jansz Visscher (c.1600).

01
Ox-eye daisies
(*Leucanthemum vulgare*)
with typical pasture
grasses.

02
German chamomile
(*Matricaria recutita*).

03
Cow parsley (*Anthriscus
sylvestris*) and buttercups
(*Ranunculus acris*).

01

02

03

or industrial facilities. There is no need to expensively ameliorate soils, for by sowing a dry meadow mix instead, mowing and management will be reduced and the kudos of helping biodiversity will reflect well on the developers.

There are other positive signs for Dutch wild flowers. One is the Room for the River programme, which by defining some land as floodwater-holding areas is reducing their attractiveness to farmers to turn them into highly fertilized ryegrass deserts. The rougher and less managed Dutch landscape of old can then re-emerge, with reeds connecting waterways with wet grassland, or the bumpy landscape of rough grazing with its tufts and tussocks

of grass and rush and occasional scrub. Most of these areas are not technically meadows, but they are a far better place for wild flowers and biodiversity than the plains of ryegrass. Small areas of woodland, or field boundaries where some trees can grow, unhindered by the endless passing of tractors or nibbling of cattle, can be great places for wild flowers too, a borderland that is neither true wood nor meadow but contains and combines many species from each.

Another development promises a new future for meadows – the realization that high productivity for grazing or even silage production does not have to mean horizon-to-horizon ryegrass. 'Herb-rich'

became something of a buzzword among farm management experts across northern Europe during the 2010s. Research is showing that having some wild flowers in with the grass increases the nutritional content of the sward, enables minerals and moisture to be drawn up from deeper in the soil and to some extent prevents the incursion of problem weeds.

Pragmatic decisions by farmers, guided by new scientific research, may yet come to the rescue of a gentler and more nature-friendly countryside.

04

04
Meadow grading into wetland near the water's edge.

05
Common yarrow (*Achillea millefolium*), heath milkwort (*Polygala serpyllifolia*), common tansy (*Tanacetum vulgare*), bush vetch (*Vicea sepium*), wild carrot (*Daucus carota*), white melilot (*Melilotus alba*), creeping thistle (*Cirsium arvense*), white bedstraw (*Gallium mollugo*), brown knapweed (*Centaurea jacea*).

06
Ribwort Plantain (*Plantago lanceolata*) can often be found with grass on high-nutrient soils.

05

06

Arjan
Boekel

The perennials sweep to the edges of the garden; there is no lawn, so this is clearly a plant lover's garden, perhaps uncompromisingly so. Near its outer limits, the surrounding fields can be seen, views of them filtered through the tall perennial stems of late summer. It is a polder landscape, north of Amsterdam, so it is lush and green, flat of course, and relatively featureless. In winter and spring, and indeed early summer, before the perennials have grown up, it must feel more exposed here, the landscape impinging on the whole property. Perennials emphasize seasonality, but they ensure that the relationship between the garden (and house) and the surrounding landscape is a seasonal one too, so in summer the garden becomes less open to the landscape and enclosed in feel, at times almost a world apart. Two aralia plants (shrubby relatives of ivy) stand silhouetted at the very edge of the garden, with few branches and big dramatic leaves; even in winter they will make a statement.

Arjan Boekel is a very plant-focused designer, but he also has a great awareness of landscape and how gardens relate to it. In another garden, the main axis is down its length but the views out are all to one side over an area of meadow grass. Views out, Arjan thinks, should not be thrust at people; it's a good thing to make them work at finding, seeing and appreciating them. 'You have to lead into the landscape through steps and straight lines but in a way which is not obvious,' he says.

In this garden, the main axis does not lead off the house, which Arjan feels would make it 'too stiff', but is at the side. Journeys should reveal their end point gradually, as with staggered steps as a way of leading from the house to the lawn. Screens such as shrubs should not directly state their function. Pollarded willows, a traditional element in polder landscapes, can be useful for this; they take time to create, although sometimes an older willow can be reshaped and pressed into service.

Slightly delaying the gaze and the feet is a good strategy in gardens that are rich in plant life; the journey needs to be slowed so that the diversity can be appreciated. Even if journeys are made every day, several times a day, there is always seasonal change and new developments: the shrub that has not flowered before, the interesting shape of developing seedheads, the short burst of deep bronze on young spring foliage.

Arjan is one of the younger generation of designers who have been born out of the so-called New Perennial movement, influenced by Piet Oudolf, Henk Gerritsen and the nurseries that became established in the 1990s, such as de Hessenhof and that of Coen Jansen. Arjan was interested in plants as a child and remembers picking flowers in his parents' garden and popping them into holes in the soil. At the age of 20 he studied landscape design at Van Hall Larenstein University of Applied Sciences while working in a nursery in his spare time, after which he went on to do a Masters degree in Landscape at the University of Wageningen before going straight into business as a garden designer.

01

03

01
A garden in the polder landscape north of Amsterdam.

02
Salvia nemorosa 'Caradonna' with scarlet *Crocosmia* 'Lucifer' and *Astrantia major* in front.

03
The small tree *Rhus typhina* with varieties of *Salvia* and wild carrot (*Daucus carota*).

04
Persicaria amplexicaulis 'Blackfield'

02

04

'In almost every garden I try to put in some new plants, so every planting scheme is different,' Arjan says. Plant diversity, of perennials at least, is at an all-time high, so there is plenty of material to work with.

Getting a good long run of seasonal interest is important to him: narcissus, alliums, and camassias in spring, trees and shrubs with colour in the autumn, not forgetting those perennials that also have

value at this time of year, such as *Aruncus* 'Horatio', with coral-red stems and good leaf colour. Hydrangeas, the cultivation of which seems to be becoming a national obsession, are not forgotten either, although perhaps favoured by Arjan more for their autumn colour than their flowers.

An enthusiasm for plants means that Arjan is aware of varieties, or of particular aspects, of plants that perhaps

other designers might not be. He enthuses about *Heptacodium miconioides* – 'Everything about it is good,' he says, 'peeling bark, foliage that looks so fresh in spring, fragrant summer flowers that leave pink calyces behind when they fall; the size is perfect for smaller gardens, too.' Although his main love is for perennials, he is more interested in woody plants than many contemporary designers. 'I am trying

05

06

08

07

05
The scarlet of scabious (*Knautia macedonica*), the widow flower, which can bloom all summer.

06
Eryngium planum 'Blauer Zwerg' and *Salvia nemorosa* 'Caradonna'.

07
The dark purple-red flowerheads seen here are *Allium sphaerocephalon*.

08
A pond margin merges with tall perennials.

09
Seedheads of *Aruncus* 'Horatio', a fine tall perennial.

09

01
Heptacodium miconioides, a small summer-flowering tree.

02
Geranium 'Rozanne', a useful late summer-flowering ground-cover variety.

03
Dark red *Sanguisorba* 'Chocolate Tip' with *Liatris spicata*.

04
Acaena microphylla, a useful ground-cover plant for the edges of paths.

05
Fern *Dryopteris erythrosora* with the foliage of *Convallaria majalis*.

01

02

03

04

05

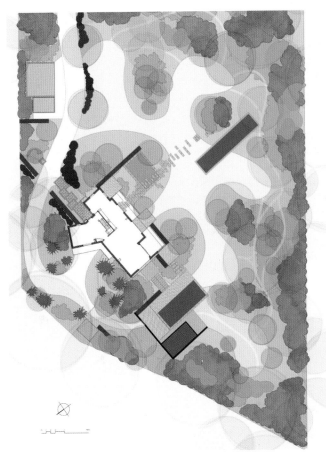

06

07

06
A path to the forested outer edges.

07
A garden design for a house in a pine and oak forest on sandy soil.

08
Liatris spicata, a good rhythm plant for the summer border.

08

to turn the wheel and use a lot more of them,' he says. He is keen on softening the edges of gardens with shrubs, or in the case of gardens in woodland, which often means pine, creating a shrub border in front of the trunks as a transition.

'Creating layering effects with shrubs and small trees is important,' he says; this enables space to be used effectively if smaller spring-flowering trees or shrubs are appropriately underplanted with perennials which will tolerate the somewhat reduced light levels and root competition.

The transition to deciduous woodland or pine forest can also be handled with a gentle gradient too, with strong-growing light shade perennials such as Japanese anemones, various *Digitalis* species, *Lunaria rediviva*, *Kirengeshoma palmata*, and ferns planted in such a way as to segue into existing wild vegetation rather than have a clear border.

Arjan has a good eye for those plants that can be most effectively repeated to create strong effects, such as the narrow purple-pink spires of *Liatris spicata* or *Geranium* 'Rozanne' used to mark out a distinct rhythm in a border, the latter's long season of relatively late flower (for a geranium and for a light shade species) making it particularly appropriate for this. In one canalside garden he designed, even *Iris sibirica* is repeated, a daring act as it's notorious for its short flowering period; however, its tidy clumps of linear foliage and chestnut-brown seedheads do not let it down during the rest of the season.

01

02

01
The flowerhead of *Aralia cashmeriana*, a relative of ivy.

02
The flower spikes of *Digitalis parviflora*.

03
Flowers of the small tree *Aralia elata*.

04
Salvia nemorosa 'Ostfriesland', ideal for dry soil.

03

05

04

06

05
Anemone × hybrida 'Dreaming Swan', which has a long late flowering season.

06
Persicaria amplexicaulis 'Rosea', which blooms for a long period in light shade.

07
Pachyphragma macrophylla, a spring-flowering shade plant.

08
Helianthus salicifolius, a relative of the common sunflower.

07

08

01

02

01
Euphorbia palustris, one of the larger early-flowering perennials.

02
Iris sibirica, whose brief flowering is followed by sturdy and attractive seedheads.

03
Iris sibirica, *Allium* 'Purple Sensation' and *Foeniculum vulgare* 'Giant Bronze'.

04
Iris sibirica and *Allium nigrum*.

05
Willow *Salix alba* with *Iris sibirica* and *Allium* 'Purple Sensation'.

03

04

In the garden which started this discussion, which was in fact his first large garden commission, he feels he was able to start working directly with plant combinations rather than filling in borders, which is what planting design is almost inevitably about in small gardens.

It is interesting to see *Helianthus salicifolius* used to unusual and spectacular effect. A very tall perennial sunflower with tightly packed very narrow leaves that never seems to flower in cultivation, which Piet Oudolf once grew but has not done so for years, it is usually seen as a rather awkward rangy border oddity. In this garden it has been planted in a number of blocks near a natural swimming pond, where it looks lushly appropriate, and far better for being en masse. 'We only had

twelve plants to begin with,' says Arjan, 'but we manage this garden like a nursery, we split plants up and move them around'.

Exploring this particular garden in late summer is a truly immersive perennial experience, with much repetition, narrow paths, tall plants, and a prairie atmosphere.

However, for early summer, *Salvia nemorosa* and its hybrids, all medium-sized herbaceous plants, are planted across the garden in a diagonal swathe. Inspired by an early Oudolf planting in a park in Sweden (the Drömparken in Enköping), it creates a dramatic early summer effect. Taller, later-flowering perennials and grasses then grow up around them, although they often flower

again later. In this garden there is a good balance between areas of intermingled, diverse planting and solid bands of one species, such as the *Helianthus*, or the solid clumps of *Persicaria amplexicaulis*. 'These are important, as they give structure,' says Arjan. Certain self-seeding species such as *Verbena bonariensis, Daucus carota* and *Knautia macedonica* ensure a continued wild and spontaneous feel, while in the autumn a large number of *Molinia caerulea* subsp. *arundinacea* plants dominate, a grass whose tall heads of tiny flowerheads and seedheads create a misty effect that makes a good background to the more defined heads of many of the perennials.

05

01

A roof terrace garden in Rotterdam uses a range of more drought-tolerant plants than would be normal for a Dutch garden. Lower-growing species are repeated across a 330 sq m (395 sq yd) terrace nine floors up, with several species of *Euphorbia* providing flower and foliage interest and grasses contributing an important element of continuity, especially the drought-tolerant mat-forming *Sesleria autumnalis* and the very tight tussocks of *Poa laballidieri*. The shallow substrate – 30 cm (12 in) at the deepest, 10 cm (4 in) around the edges – presented difficulties, so Arjan took the unconventional step of seeding in the more difficult areas, with species such as *Centranthus ruber*, thinking that in this way a process of natural selection would result in the most appropriate plants for the conditions surviving. Indeed they have, and the survivors then self-seeded elsewhere. 'It was a really dry summer the first year after planting,' says Arjan, 'and we wanted to minimize irrigation. It was incredible to see how everything came back to life in the autumn.'

With such a wide range of plants now available, the future for imaginative plant-orientated designers like Arjan looks bright. Perennials and grasses in strong and innovative combinations, but not forgetting the important but recently rather overlooked element of woody plants, suggests plenty to look forward to.

02

03

04

01
A roof garden in Rotterdam. The pink flowers are *Saponaria officinalis*.

02
The rusty fading flowerheads of *Euphorbia amygdaloides* 'Purpurea'.

03
Digitalis parviflora, short-lived but self-seeding.

04
Allium senescens, a relatively short and late-flowering species.

05
Pink *Dianthus carthusianorum* with purple *Erysimum* 'Bowles Mauve'.

05

GARDENS UNDER BIG SKIES

INSPIRED BY CULTURAL LANDSCAPES

BULBFIELDS

Coaches pull up, people get out, many of them with cameras at the ready, and gather en masse at the edges of the fields. Welcome to tulip tourism. The bulbfields of western Holland are one of Europe's great tourist sights, playing a significant part in attracting some of the 16 million-plus visitors the country has every year. The sight is surreal: a landscape as ordered and disciplined as any in a country where the agricultural land is always tidy and intentional, but where the long rectangular fields are usually green with lush grass or other crops, or studded with cows, these are instead painted with brightly coloured flowers. Only for a few spring months, though, from late January when the crocuses come out, to May with the tulips – the rest of the year they are mainly green or bare, although there may be some summer gladioli, lilies and dahlias later on.

The first thought of the visitor might be that this is like an artwork, where the humdrum green of ordinary crops is somehow transformed into something aesthetic and spectacular; the geometric slabs of primary colours of a Piet Mondrian painting, perhaps. However, on walking around more and looking across the fields, it is clear that this is not the case. This is just commercial horticulture, so the colours adjacent to each other might sometimes clash, and there are big gaps where there are no flowers to be seen. All the bulbs are grouped into quite narrow beds, so that they fit between the wheels of a tractor. It is plain that this is a very businesslike way of organizing the landscape and the business here is flower bulbs. They are grown for parks and gardens, not just in The Netherlands but, thanks to a powerful brand linking of 'Dutch' and 'bulbs', all over the world. That hundreds of thousands of visitors descend every year to look at them is almost incidental.

There are many different ways of viewing the tulips. Most visitors travel by coach, while the more energetic can cycle,

01

02

03

04

and it being The Netherlands, with plenty of water, there is tulip-viewing from boats too. Visitors from all over the world are brought here by tulips, but go on to experience more Dutch culture in the towns where they stay, and like much culture packaged for tourists, they are fed plenty of clichés: windmills, clogs, women in bonnets, big round cheeses.

Elsewhere in the country, in less romantic places like Flevoland, flat even by Dutch standards of flatness and reclaimed

from the sea only about 70 years ago, there are tulips too – an increasing number every year, for they, and other bulbs, are a remunerative crop, earning more than grass, wheat or potatoes. The world wants tulips, and they want their tulips to be Dutch. Every year, for example, a buyer from Huis ten Bosch, a Dutch theme park in Nagasaki, Japan, pays a visit to decide what varieties to get for next year's display. To buy anything other than Dutch would be unthinkable. Meanwhile in China, big

tulip displays are increasingly popular in public parks, although if news reports are to be believed, many visitors have not yet learnt that they are not supposed to wade in and cut the flowers. So to meet demand, the bulb-growing area is spreading way beyond the traditional Bollenstreek fields in the west – even far-away Drenthe, in the north of the country, is turning to bulb production.

05

06

07

08

01

02

03

Tulips and Holland

Tulip tourism is an add-on for a country that produces around three-quarters of the world's flower bulbs, most of which are tulips – around three billion annually. The Netherlands, and the provinces of North and South Holland in particular, are inextricably linked to the tulip, which has become the number one national symbol. Tulip iconography is everywhere, especially in anything to do with the tourist industry, where representations of the flower seem to sprout colourfully on websites, restaurant tables, shopfronts and much else. Behind the modern tulip lies a tale in which the core event, the so-called tulip mania of the period 1634–37, has become not just one of those items of history that everyone seems to have heard about, but one that is still much disputed by economic historians – in particular just how irrational it was, or indeed was not.

Tulips had been introduced into northern Europe some one hundred years earlier from the Ottoman Empire (the core of which is modern Turkey), along with hyacinths, which also attracted the attention of speculators. Although still theoretically under Spanish rule, the Dutch had been building up an extremely successful economy, largely through trade. Many of the key aspects of modern capitalism were invented in Amsterdam – for example, the city had the world's

first full-time stock exchange. Given the country's geography, investment in land (the investment of choice for the nouveau riche the world over) was difficult, so money had to seek other routes to grow. Tulips were one such speculative investment – they became status symbols for the newly rich merchant and financier class, which stimulated both a rise in prices and efforts to breed ever more exquisite blooms. The bulbs which were most sought after were those which were infected with the tulip-breaking potyvirus, which caused a pattern of elaborate streaking in the petals. As far as the breeder was concerned, a tulip was only as good as its infection, which, since there was no understanding of either genetics or the existence of viruses, had to be left entirely to chance. Desperate measures were tried, with one grower tying together half a red tulip bulb and half a white in an attempt to get striped flowers.

As the love of tulips grew and grew, so did the prices, with particularly fine bulbs regularly reaching hundreds of florins, at a time when a pig might cost only 30. In 1636 a 'Semper Augustus' bulb sold for 6,000 florins. Given the inventiveness of financiers, who had made a lot of the wealth of Amsterdam possible, it is not surprising that a futures market developed – in bulbs not even planted, let alone blooming. With tulips being traded on stock markets and the less wealthy members of society joining in, a speculative bubble soon grew. When traders could no longer get the prices they wanted for their bulbs, the bubble burst, and many were ruined.

'Tulipmania is seen as part of the Dutch way of trading,' says Jacqueline van der Kloet, a garden designer who has become the modern face of gardening with bulbs, 'no joke, no embarrassment. The Dutch always have been traders and have taken risks every now and then. So yes, you could say that they were behaving in a way they thought was right, though of course it included a lot of gambling.'

We might look at the world and say that an awful lot that happens is irrational. The Dutch tulip industry is a particularly good example. At first sight it would seem as if The Netherlands is almost the worst possible place to grow tulips. Plants of the genus *Tulipa* come overwhelmingly from the Middle East and Central Asia; botanists would regard the latter region with its extremes of cold winters and hot summers as the richest source. Springs are short, and succeeded by long dry summers. Why would a country famous for having problems with drainage, and a cool maritime climate, become the place to develop, grow and market a plant from central Asia?

The answer lies in history. When it was introduced, the flower just happened to be the right thing at the right time for a culture that was experimenting with a range of novel financial and commercial mechanisms, as well as being highly innovative in the visual arts. As to how the Dutch were able to cultivate them, this

04

05

is a matter of geography. Tulips have long been grown in the Bollenstreek, the 'bulb strip', a band of land parallel to the coast which stretches from Haarlem in the north (more or less parallel to Amsterdam) to near Leiden in the south. The Bollenstreek lies just behind a line of sand dunes which runs along the coast. Sand, as any gardener will tell you, is not generally an ideal material in which to grow plants; it does not hold water, so plants dry out very quickly. However, for growing plants from a region with dry soils, this is no bad thing, and in the case of tulips a positive good one. Bulbs generally are liable to rot in wet soils and tulips particularly so. Growers early in the history of the bulb industry soon realized that land in the lee of the dunes, where sand had been excavated for use in building, was good for the plants, especially if the sand were mixed in with just enough clay, peat or other material that would help it hold a little more moisture and, crucially, supply nutrients, for tulips are greedy growers. The lime in the sand, the result of long-dead shells, created good conditions of soil chemistry for bulbs too. The resulting complex and artificial soil has long been known as 'geestgrond'.

The late 19th century saw much urban development, which needed a lot of sand; it also saw Dutch bulbs become an international commodity, and advances in plant breeding that made the tulip not just a special plant for pots but something to plant out en masse.

The levelled dunes were ideal for a new, and far more serious, phase of tulip-growing to feed the increasing popularity of bulb displays in parks and gardens across both Europe and North America. It was this era that saw the long rectangles of brilliant colour appear in the spring landscape.

Agriculture, whether growing grass, cows or tulips, means eliminating what was there before. It is an ethical conundrum these days, another potential battleground between business and conservation.

There are very few dune grasslands left. There is an irony here in that these grasslands, sparse and windswept, have played a key part in trapping the grains of sand blown in by the sea, which made the dunes that protected the land from the raging water. Some areas of degraded grassland, though, are being restored and some are being actively managed as water catchment areas, the grassland, soil and sand acting as filters for the water needed by the country's cities.

01
An allegory of spring in an 18th-century engraving.

02
A Delft polychrome tulip vase, c.1710, with places for eight flowers.

03
Floral Still Life, by Hans Bollongier (1639). The tulips are 'Semper Augustus'.

04
A cartoon of the tulip trade made in 1637, depicting the Goddess Flora in a land yacht. She is a personification of vain hope of profit.

05
Page from a tulip book, by Jacob Marrel, c.1640, possibly a catalogue or inventory.

Jacqueline van der Kloet

INSPIRED BY CULTURAL LANDSCAPES

Travellers to the bulb fields invariably also go to Keukenhof, a 32-hectare (79-acre) park around a historic castle, with what is probably the most spectacular floral exhibition garden in the world. The bulb planting started in 1949 as a way of showing off the country's bulb industry – a kind of glorified trade show. Today, more than a million visitors a year admire bed after bed of flowers, mostly dominated by tulips. Traditionally, these beds, which can involve an annual planting of around seven million bulbs, have been not just intensely colourful but sternly regimented, all the bowl-shaped tulip blooms at exactly the same height, marching in their serried ranks in beds that snake up and down and curve around under the trees of the historic parkland. Among gardeners, the Keukenhof displays became a byword for a particular model of highly controlled and precisely choreographed horticultural spectacle. Those in the gardening world who consider themselves sophisticated look on askance; Keukenhof is definitely a populist spectacle. Since 2005, however, Keukenhof has been making changes, with some more informal planting and a much wider range of non-bulbous plants. The results are softer, calmer, more romantic and in a funny way actually show the tulips off better; no longer is the eye blinded by masses of colour, but instead sees more of the individual flowers, with the chance to compare and contrast and see tulips counterposed with other plants.

Keukenhof's new face is the result of the involvement of Jacqueline van der Kloet, a garden designer who has been involved extensively with bulbs since 1993. Rather than planting tulips at precisely measured distances as was previously the case, Jacqueline adopted a method which earlier Keukenhof designers might have regarded as sacrilege, throwing bulbs up in the air and planting them where they fell. The result is that the concentrations of tulips vary – some patches are denser and others thinner, just as is the case with the wild flowers in any natural habitat. The tulips are interspersed with perennials, some grown primarily for flowers such as violas, while others such *Brunnera macrophylla* 'Variegata' are chosen for their foliage.

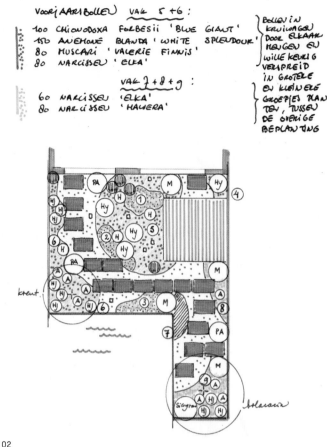

01

02

In 2012, Jacqueline handed over to younger designers, but she now undertakes similar integrated bulb plantings in other public gardens, both here and abroad, with her work being appreciated in Chicago's Lurie Garden and at Huis ten Bosch, the Dutch-styled theme park in Japan.

'The old-fashioned way of using bulbs,' says Jacqueline, 'was digging a number of holes in the border and filling them with red tulips, yellow daffodils, blue hyacinths, preferably in that kind of combination, regardless of the situation and whatever the surrounding plants were – or planting a line of daffodils or tulips along the driveway, for example one tulip or daffodil every 10 centimetres. My sources of inspiration were alpine meadows with their abundance of flowers, among which are many bulbs.' As a garden designer Jacqueline has been very influenced by the English gardener Gertrude Jekyll, who used drifts of plants in combinations built around colour. 'My style involves more mixing of plants, though,' she says. 'I visited a lot of English gardens picking up ideas for colour schemes.'

The apparent randomization of planting combined with the careful choice of colours is applied not just to tulips but to a wide range of bulbs, with Jacqueline's projects showing a range of adventurous approaches, often with effects that manage to be at once electrifying and harmonious. One example combines a mix of several varieties of grape hyacinths (Muscari) in different shades of blue filling formal borders, while another brings together varieties of crocus and chionodoxa with flowers of similar colours but very different forms. Startlingly innovative ways of introducing bulbs to gardens may be used as well, such as a sinuous line of mixed anemones and tulips snaking across the grass of a very geometrically formal garden, with some tulips even popping up through the low clipped yew hedging.

While The Netherlands has the reputation for being the world's leading plant producer, planting design was historically weakly developed compared to what happened in the country's gardening neighbours, Germany and Britain. Jacqueline's career as a garden designer

has been at a time when international influences have been strong. 'I trained as a garden and landscape architect, then worked for a company that designed and made gardens in Amsterdam, where I designed many public or semi-public spaces and the occasional private garden,' she says. 'I worked there for six years, then started my own business because I really liked designing private gardens and I loved making elaborate plant schemes. In the same period I started the garden in Weesp.

01
Pinkish forget-me-not (Myosotis), leaf of Geranium macrorrhizum 'Spessart', tulip 'Flaming Spring Green', flower of Geranium macrorrhizum 'Spessart', tulip 'Jacqueline', Allium roseum, Allium triquetrum, leaf of Helleborus orientalis, Geranium pratense 'Album', leaf of Geranium pratense 'Album', Stipa tenuissima, black widow (Geranium phaeum), blue forget-me-not (Myosotis).

02
A plan for a small garden.

03
Tulips 'Queen of Night', 'Menton' and 'Angelique' with Euphorbia cyparissias and forget-me-not (Myosotis sylvatica).

03

De Theetuin (The Tea Garden) is an English-inspired garden which Jacqueline set up with some friends in Weesp, a small city just east of Amsterdam where they continue to live.

It is open to the public, and, she says, 'It gives me an opportunity to show in reality the combinations of plants I like to create, so the garden more or less acts as a living business card.'

Jacqueline's use of bulbs really took off in 1993 after the former International Flower Bulb Centre (IFBC) asked her to write some magazine articles about bulbs, supplying her with plentiful samples the autumn before. She explains, 'I decided to plant them in the same way that I had planted the perennials: in mixed groups, scattered in between other plants. The results were marvellous and that was the start of my working with bulbs.' The relationship with the IFBC continued, with Jacqueline promoting her bulb-planting style as well as making an ongoing evaluation of the plants' long-term performance; in particular, she noted which tulip varieties continued to flower year after year, as many are 'one-year wonders' only.

01

02

03

01
Grass Milium effusum 'Aureum', Geranium sylvaticum 'Amy Doncaster'.

02
Allium 'Purple Sensation', one of the ornamental garlics.

03
Tulip 'Recreado' with Geranium tuberosum.

04
An overview of the
Theetuin.

05
Tulips 'Black Hero' and
'Spring Green'.

06
Tulip 'Passionale' with
hostas, hellebores and
box balls.

04

06

05

01

INSPIRED BY CULTURAL LANDSCAPES

01
Tulips 'Jacqueline' and 'Mariette', Geranium *macrorrhizum* 'Spessart', and in the background *Viburnum plicatum* 'Watenabe'.

02
Yellow *Smyrnium perfoliatum*, tulip 'Ballerina' and the small round tree in the background is *Ligustrum delavayanum*.

03
Smyrnium perfoliatum, a privet hedge, and steps to the dyke with some of the neighbouring sheep.

04
Tulips 'Ballerina', 'Daydream', 'Flashback' and 'Ronaldo'.

05
Smyrnium perfoliatum and tulip 'Ballerina'.

02

03

05

04

01
Camassia leichtlinii, an increasingly popular prairie species.

02
Creeping shade-lover *Brunnera macrophylla* 'Sea Heart'.

03
Summer-flowering *Gladiolus callianthus* 'Murielae'.

04
Flowers of the very variable *Geranium phaeum*.

05
The evergreen *Euphorbia amygdaloides* var. *robbiae*.

06
Snowdrop *Galanthus elwesii*.

07
Clerodendron trichotomum, a small tree with fragrant flowers.

08
Fritillaria persica 'Ivory Bells', a white form of this usually dark purple flowering bulbous plant.

09
Tulipa turkestanica, one of the 'species' group of tulips.

01

02

Mixing tulips and other bulbs with other plants relies on choosing varieties which complement the bulbs. Often this involves selecting flowering perennials with colours and shapes that either contrast or harmonize, but since most perennials do not flower until later in the summer, foliage is as important as flowers, if not more so, in making these choices. When the first snowdrops and crocuses emerge most perennials are still dormant, but when the last tulips, alliums and poeticus daffodils perform, several months later, the range of actively growing perennials will be very much greater, and the planting will be on the cusp of extensive perennial flowering. A smooth 'hand-over' is important, with perennials taking over from bulbs but without crowding them out.

Of course bulbs are not limited to spring, especially if we extend the word 'bulb' to all those plants that can be grown from discrete dry storage organs (the 'geophytes' of the botanist). Increasingly, Jacqueline has been experimenting with using dahlias alongside annuals and perennials, their defined shapes offering concentrated colours alongside the often hazier forms of plants such as purple *Verbena bonariensis* or those with smaller scattered flowers, for example yellow *Rudbeckia fulgida*.

She now also works for a company to design summer seasonal plantings for French municipalities and also for others who want flower displays for high-visibility locations such as public spaces or parks.

Lilies *(Lilium spp.)* and the smaller more graceful *Gladiolus* join cultivars of *Ixia, Sparaxis, Zantedeschia*, and many others combined with annuals to ring the changes from year to year. The possibilities for exuberant summer plantings are enormous, especially with new cultivars and the ability to choose unconventional planting combinations and make them work, which Jacqueline seems able to do remarkably well. To have a fresh eye, unencumbered by received wisdom, for putting plants together is her real gift.

Among the perennials which Jacqueline favours for her naturalistic combinations are varieties of *Brunnera macrophylla*, with broad leaves that emerge early and sprays of tiny forget-me-not flowers (usually blue but sometimes white) that appear at the same time as those of many bulbs, along with varieties of the related *Pulmonaria* with leaves often splashed with silver and notably early pink or blue flowers. She uses several *Euphorbia* for its yellow-green flowers that will complement almost any other colour, such as the relatively low-growing shade-tolerant *E. amygdaloides*.

Otherwise, she favours mostly foliage which sits alongside the bulbs. Species of *Geranium* nearly always leaf up early, as do *Alchemilla mollis*, species of *Amsonia*, *Aquilegia* and *Erysimum* and *Pachyphragma macrophylla*. Some foliage emerges later, to coincide only with the later bulbs, but nevertheless offers opportunities such as the emerging 'noses' of hostas or the dark bronze-red of young peony foliage, the latter looking particularly striking alongside blue scillas.

03

04

05

06

07

08

09

01

01
Gladiolus callianthus
'Murielae' and *Coreopsis*
tripteris.

02
The white flowers of
Gladiolus callianthus
'Murielae'.

03
Dahlia 'Ellen Houston'.

04
Dahlia 'Ellen Houston'
with the grass *Imperata*
cylindrica 'Rubra' (syn.
'Red Baron').

02

03

04

05, 06, 08
Dahlia 'Moonshine'

07
Gladiolus callianthus
'Murielae'.

05

06

07

08

GARDENS UNDER BIG SKIES

01

01
Dahlia 'Chat Noir'.

02
Verbena bonariensis,
Verbena rigida 'Polaris',
Salvia farinacea 'Cirrus',
Cleome spinosa 'Sparkler
Rose', *Dahlia* 'Papa'.

03
Lobelia × *speciosa*
'Starship Scarlet'

04
Dahlia 'Happy
Single Wink'

05
A mixture of summer-
flowering bulbs and
annuals.

02

04

03

05

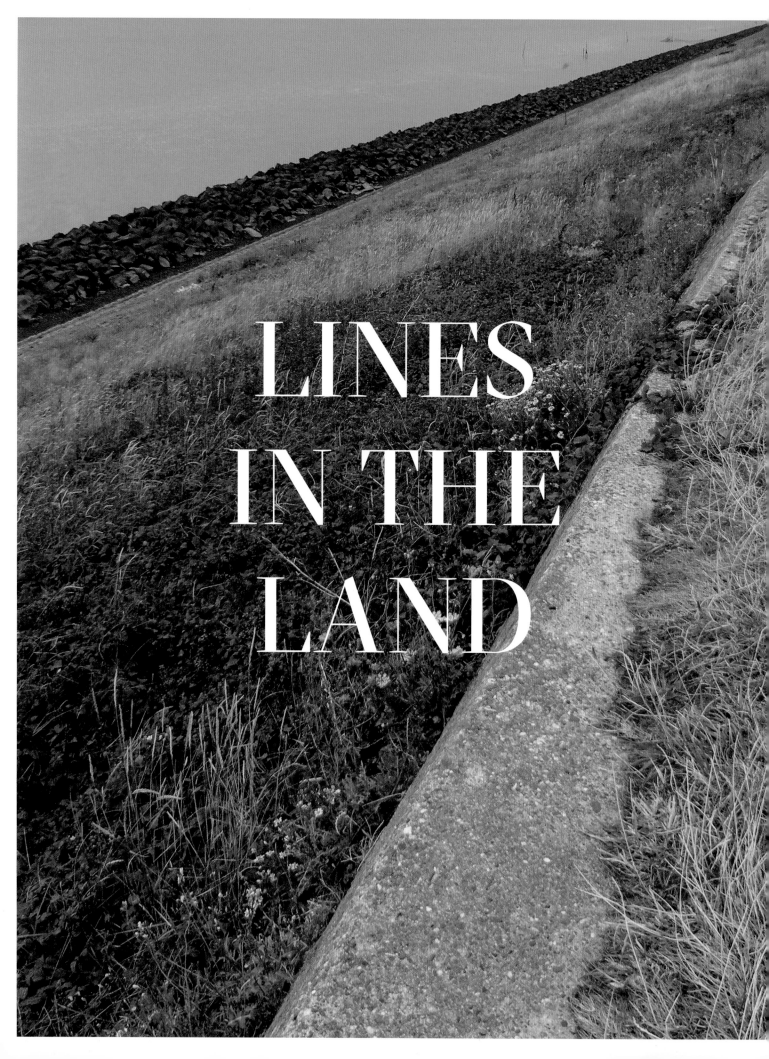

LINES
IN THE
LAND

Driving across the Afsluitdijk can be a surreal experience, especially in fog, where the road sweeps, as straight as the proverbial arrow, into a grey nothingness. Even in summer when the weather is clear when you set off, it is not entirely apparent where you will end up. On a causeway with water on both sides, you might feel a bit as if you are on a ship. The reality is very different, as you are in fact on a barrier, with sea water on one side and fresh on the other, although if the weather is calm this distinction is not apparent to the eye.

The Afsluitdijk, which means enclosure dyke, is often seen as the crowning glory of the Dutch battle against the sea. The Delta projects which have now safeguarded the south-west of the country against flooding may be, in engineering terms, more complex and more advanced, but in terms of sheer brazen boldness and drama the Afsluitdijk is hard to beat. As a landscape feature it transforms geographical perceptions, since two different parts of the country which once could only communicate by ship (Noord Holland and Friesland) are connected, and it has turned what was an extended bay of the sea into what is effectively a lake, the IJselmeer. As well as acting to protect a large area of the country from the incursion of the sea, it has enabled new polders to be created, with an enormous expansion of agricultural land, so the Afsluitdijk is seen as part of a larger project usually dubbed the Zuiderzee Works after the bay that previously existed here. While its status as the world's longest such barrier, with a length of 32 km (20 miles) has now ceded to the Saemangeum Seawall Project in South Korea, this still must be the world's boldest ever landscaping project.

The construction between 1927 and 1932, the preparatory work beforehand and the development work on the land afterwards, was a great national project. Members of the public could subscribe to a regular report issued by the government department concerned in the form of a well-produced journal outlining the project and keeping readers up to date with progress, with detailed descriptions of the works, illustrated with photographs, maps and diagrams.

01
The plan for the enclosure of polders in the IJsselmeer.

02
One of a series of booklets produced by the government: *The closure and partial reclamation of the Zuiderzee*, (No. XI, 1926).

03
Willow withies being used in the construction of a dyke slope.

04
'Mattresses' of willow used to support stones in an early stage of dyke construction.

The tone of national confidence and of 'man against nature' was typical of the time, similar to American reports of the construction of dam projects in the Western states and to Soviet publications of the period outlining great irrigation and agricultural schemes, though shorn of the latter's ideology. With the completion of the Afsluitdijk in 1932, one world ended and another began. The enclosure of the waters of the Zuiderzee shut off the route that had historically been taken by both shipping and fishing boats to the towns that were dotted along its banks. An arm of the sea became a freshwater lake.

The Afsluitdijk is an enormous and obvious feature, and with water on both sides, it dominates the landscape. The vast majority of dykes, however, are more subtle, often nothing more than a ridge in the landscape. Most are covered in grass, so they are not easy to see, and it is often a road or cycle track along the top that first draws attention to them. In fact, it takes some time for the visitor to really get their eye in, but once they do they will see them everywhere. Dykes, by keeping back water, very often from land which is below sea level, have made this country. They also make up a lot of what we see in the landscape. There are dykes for many purposes: to keep back the sea, to keep rivers in their courses, to

direct canals, to act as backup if another is breached, to ensure the drainage of a polder, and old defence dykes to allow flooding to prevent invasion. A great many are historic, and may not serve a function any more.

As well as being a crucial visual part of the landscape, dykes are the means by which the landscape can exist. Seeing them on a map tends to make us think of them as being like a web, and indeed they can also be seen as a system of communication.

Since so many have roads or cycleways along their tops they become a means by which we can explore the landscape, and in so doing get something of a better view through our elevated position.

These are lines in the landscape that serve many functions. In old landscapes, where dykes were dug by hand and every piece of safeguarded land was the fruit of human labour, the dykes and the areas they enclose tend to be small and irregular. Landscapes are intimate and complex, as old, often eroded and now usually purposeless dykes criss-cross and intermesh. The result can be a pleasantly confusing series of spaces and elevations, much of the landforms being the fossilized remains of many centuries

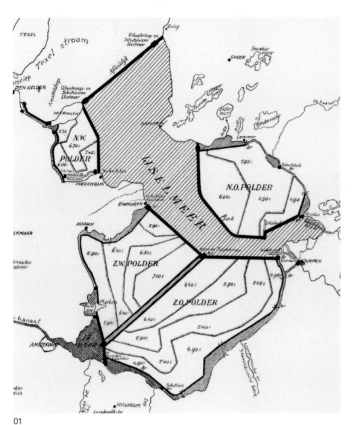

01

02

03

of digging and draining, and all too often flooding and redraining. New landscapes, such as those of the land reclaimed from the Zuiderzee, like the vast Flevopolder, involve a very low ratio of dyke to land; everything is rationally planned and roads and boundaries are straight, although the enclosing dyke rarely is so for long, as it has to follow natural and historic coastlines or water courses. The contrast between the old and the new landscape is dramatic.

The ruthless rationality of the government bodies responsible for drainage and flood protection has meant that sometimes these two visions of the landscape, the old and complex, the modern and simplified, have come into conflict. The destruction of historic dykes, houses and even whole villages aroused much opposition during the 1970s.

The engineers' vision of a super-safe country with all dangers rationalized out of existence was not to everyone's taste; the opposition of nature-lovers to the destruction of habitats was joined with the opposition of those who wished to preserve heritage, or just felt dislocated by the ripping up of the familiar.

04

In an extraordinary twist of fate, the Oostvaardersplassen, an area in the new landscape of Flevoland, in the southern part of the reclaimed Zuiderzee, has become one of the world's most acclaimed and discussed examples of rewilding – the return of landscapes to unmanaged nature. The 22 sq km² (8½ sq mile) area was sown with reed seed from planes, and so became a wildlife-rich marsh. Too sandy for agriculture, it had been earmarked for greenhouses but, after campaigning by biologists, in the 1970s it acquired the designation of 'temporary nature reserve', a status which eventually become permanent. Various animals were introduced, such as primitive breeds of cattle and horses, and a policy of zero management followed. The result has attracted much interest and controversy. Many trees are ring-barked by hungry animals, so they die, and the ensuing 'untidy' landscape challenges our conceptions of what 'nature' and 'natural' landscapes are like. The mere existence of such a place would probably have horrified the engineer creators of the Zuiderzee Works, but landscape history here has a way of turning full circle.

01

02

03

04

05

06

07

01
The Afsluitdijk.

02
A flood control canal.

03
Remains of the churchyard of Oterdum near Delfzijl, the old village that was demolished in the construction of a widened dyke along the Zeehavenkanaal.

04
The Verdronken Land van Saeftinghe – the 'drowned land'.

05
Aardenburg, in Zeeland, a landscape of ancient, hand-dug dykes.

06
The Reitdiep, the old river connection between the city of Groningen and the Lauwersmeer.

07
Pumping station Sichterman, near Winsum, Groningen.

08
The river Lek at Vianen and its floodplain.

09
Heck cattle in the Oostvaardersplassen.

10
Sea holly (*Eryngium maritimum*) on the Afsluitdijk.

08

INSPIRED BY CULTURAL LANDSCAPES

10

Luc
Engelhard

Garden designer Luc Engelhard's own garden brings together the wild and the designed, with many juxtapositions between the two. In his professional capacity he is not particularly a 'wild gardener', but in his 2 hectares (5 acres) of former agricultural smallholding in a classic polder landscape south of Utrecht, he has the extremes of both, sometimes brought together, sometimes kept apart.

The garden is a testing ground for ideas, and feels almost a laboratory, with experiments and prototypes dotted around every corner. 'I made the garden here as an experimental place,' he says, 'it is always changing. It's a place to bring potential clients, after which they usually say that they trust me.'

The garden is a rather elongated rectangle, a typical shape for a polder plot. The surrounding landscape feels ever present as there are many views out between the boundary trees, and as Luc points out, 'In a polder landscape you always have to work with it – the garden is here because of the polder, it is part of it.' Luc's house, a glasshouse, a studio building and outbuildings are all on an axis in line with the long side of the plot perimeter. A large pool dominates the end nearest the road, just outside Luc's studio. A line of pillars made from piled-up cut sections of old paving slabs march along one side, becoming progressively more spaced out from one side to the other. The contrast with the lush waterside vegetation, such as the large-leaved *Petasites japonicus*, is dramatic. Though the pillars serve no function, they somehow look as if they should, a nod to Luc's fascination with follies which readers of his blog can't help but notice. They make a striking intervention, and of course in the depths of winter will be all the more valued.

'I built the house in 1995,' says Luc. 'It plays with the environment. I made a glasshouse too, using glass offcuts, so the panes are all different sizes – it's a Piet Mondrian glasshouse. In other buildings I've used concrete, steel, old bricks . . . for me the connections between art, architecture and plants are very important.' The glasshouse's somewhat irregular arrangement of reused panes sets it apart from the regularity of the commercial structures that are so familiar. It contains a small number of plants and can be used as a display space, for example for exhibitions of ceramics. Its paving is clearly set at a different angle to the right angles of the sides; some display staging is set on this angle too, in line with a yew hedge outside, so there are two very clear overlapping visual frameworks.

The effect is very powerful, creating the sensation of being in two places at once. Outside, the corner of the hedge juts out across the line of the track which runs down parallel to the side of the glasshouse. The fact that it is neither parallel to the track nor at right angles makes a strong impression too. This skilful playing with geometries to create surprises will be familiar to anyone who has seen much of the work of Mien Ruys.

'It was the 1980s and I wanted somewhere in the countryside,' says Luc of his decision to come here. 'I grew up with the cows in the countryside, but my parents had a cultural background. I started working on farms, but was unsure about what to study. I realised I was not an artist, I was too grounded.'

He ended up studying horticulture and garden design. 'Gardens at the time (the 1970s) were very dominated by conifers,' Luc says. 'The only designer not using them was Mien Ruys, who was a great discovery. She was the only garden architect who attracted my attention, and was the turning point for me.' He went on to develop a successful career in garden-making and construction, but often felt frustrated by what he felt was the 'slow' progress of garden architecture; 'Apart from Mien Ruys, there was nothing in gardening until the mid-1990s, and then we kicked out the conifers.' 'As a young man, I was fascinated by Braque, Picasso, Leger,' he says, 'I encountered Bauhaus when I was 25, but I was also fascinated by plants, which I studied, evening after evening, Sunday after Sunday.'

Luc remembers the first Piet Oudolf open day, an event in 1984 when Piet hosted the first of many days where other nurseries were invited to have stalls, which became very effective meeting places for a new generation of gardeners. Luc went on to run a business which by the 1990s had ten to twelve employees. The International Garden Show (IGA) in Munich in 1986 was clearly a seminal event. He says, 'It's always in my memory. There was a lot of cement, different surfaces of concrete – we experienced it as art, as well as good planting. I loved the interactions with plants. I took all my employees, and we all learnt so much.' Other inspirations have been the British environmental artist Andy Goldsworthy. Luc says, 'He touches something; his work has become a part of me. I show his books to clients, and they always like what he does.' Other inspirations have been the gardens of the International Garden Festival at Chaumont-sur-Loire in France and the landscape and architecture of the Museum Insel Hombroich. Luc's garden certainly references the latter's oddly random collection of quirky but restrained architecture and sculpture scattered around 21 hectares (52 acres) of low-lying meadowland.

Willow is a sculptural material of which Luc is fond; he enjoys its flexibility. There is plenty of pollarding here but also an extraordinary screen made of willow wands growing in a cross-shaped pattern, the union of each 'x' holding a substantial log of wood. He suggests that other trees can be shaped too, although they are inevitably less flexible: *Liquidambar, Parrotia, Cercis siliquastrum, Amelanchier*.

The coming together of modern materials such as concrete with clean, simple lines is greatly complemented by Luc's choice of plants. Areas around buildings are usually planted with species which have a real chunky, graphic quality, such as ferns, grasses and large-leaved *Persicaria* species. It is somewhat telling that Luc waxes lyrical about *Festuca mairei*, a rather underrated grass of which he says 'Its design quality mainly lies in its dense, bushy form with its robust, powerful appearance, going well together with hard elements and cropped shapes.'

Beyond the buildings much of the planting is lighter in tone, with a lot of grasses, and grass and perennial mixtures. Real wildness takes over towards the furthest end, where a large pool is surrounded by reedmace, willows and alders.

01

03

01
Meadow grass and a
pergola in a client's
garden.

02
A gap in this brushwood
hedge looks through to
the fields.

03
Logs held in the crux of
willow crosses with tufted
hair grass (*Deschampsia
cespitosa*).

04
A concrete pier has
many uses.

05
A concrete basin beneath
old pear trees.

04

05

06

07

08

09

06
Unfolding fronds of royal
fern (*Osmunda regalis*).

07
Gunnera manicata, which
has the largest leaves of
any hardy plant.

08
Goldenrod (*Solidago*)
and wild flowers.

09
A simple timber bridge
leads out to the fields.

01

02

03

04

05

01
Pollarded willows
merging with the water.

02
Phlomis tuberosa
emerging from lavender.

03
A plan by Luc Engelhard.

04
Individually cast concrete
slabs and mini-ditches.

05
Mazus miquelii, one of the
very low ground-covers
Luc likes to use between
stones.

Concrete does not always need to have clean lines, however, and Luc is fond of experimenting with it in various ways which turn it into a much rougher and more irregular material. He has a technique of making water basins so the outside is very rough and 'there are points where it weeps water so moss and grass can grow, but these points are unpredictable'. The results are a little like an ersatz version of the tufa beloved of 18th-century grotto-makers.

Just before the really wild marshland part of the garden takes over, there is a pool with an example of a design trope that

seems to appear in a lot of Luc's work – a sturdy straight line, a bit like a modern dyke, but apparently made of cement blocks . . . but it ends, and so what appears to be a division of some kind (and in this context is what most of us would read as a dam holding back water) is revealed as a visual device. It has the unexpected quality that is perhaps one of the most distinctive elements of Mien Ruys's work. A similar effect appears in a garden Luc designed, where a line of massive stones crosses the garden but with a wide break to walk through. 'Every stone was a sculpture,' he says. 'We had to work

with the stones as they came, rather than specifying them. Sculpting with them was a challenge.' In another garden, a line of cement cubes cuts across a pond, but with a break that allows water to tumble down to another level.

Cement or stone appears frequently, but nearly always in a way that is almost reticent. Slabs for walking are usually laid so that there are gaps for plants to grow through – marginal plants if by water, carefully chosen groundcovers such as the blue-flowered *Mazus reptans* if on dry land.

06

07

06
Pillars made from old
paving slabs in Luc's pond.

07
Re-used paving cobbles
allow for plenty of small
plants to grow.

08
A subtle garden
boundary made with
uncompromising material.

08

01
Old timbers make
a bridge.

02
Water-management
barriers made ornamental.

03
A boardwalk for those
with good balance.

01

02

Gardens in the country are very often in a close relationship to water, especially in polder landscapes. Indeed the closeness of the water level in canals to the ground level is something that soon impresses itself on visitors. 'All the time we have to work with water,' says Luc. 'Levels can go up and down – sometimes the water authorities drop the level to get more oxygen into the soil for the farmers.' The smallest change in level can result in quite big changes in vegetation, with the highest water level supporting reeds *(Phragmites australis)*, the most visually dominating (and competitively spreading) plant. 'To some extent you can play with the water levels,' explains Luc. 'You can make a swimming pool that is just above the level of the water. But water is dangerous, so anyone working with it has to know what they are doing. Many Dutch people are afraid of it, and some build their houses higher than they need to be because of that. A designer can take the water of the polder to the threshold of the house or keep it at a distance.'

It is also possible to take the garden owner out into the water, as with the reed-fringed pool at the end of Luc's garden. This includes a rather frightening boardwalk from one side to another, three slightly rickety-looking planks wide. Luc says, 'In summer you could be walking through the reeds at 10 cm (4 in) above the water line. Usually there is a rail but there isn't one here, so it is quite challenging – but it gets people talking about water.' This is daring, as some of these people will be potential clients, whom Luc always invites to his garden so that they can see what he does.

In one garden, near the river Vecht, Luc has used the fact that the water level may change as a feature in its own right. 'There are two qualities of the water's behaviour in the polder: fluctuations by rain and by pumping,' he says. A terrace of stone setts with oak beams backs onto the house and beyond it is a canal. Luc explains, 'I used the high oak beams and put them at a height at which they are sometimes in the water and sometimes just out of it, depending on the level. I deliberately used a strip of beams to attract attention to their function, which is to show the water level. Sometimes it even swirls vigorously when water is being pumped to the river Vecht. So when it has rained a lot the beams can be partly submerged and when pumping is under way they will be out of the water.'

The very nature of the polder integrates land and water, and makes the garden a product of its landscape. Luc's skill as a garden designer is about recognizing this and playing inventively with all the possibilities of this intrinsically Dutch relationship.

03

FLOODING: FLEE OR FIGHT?

The *Waterlinie* (Waterline) is a paradox, but then visitors to The Netherlands should be used to paradoxes and puzzles by the time they discover it. Nevertheless, a land where water and earth seem somehow inverted should continue to surprise. The Waterline is one of the biggest single historical landscape features in the country, and yet it is not actually visible as such, only pieces of it, and they often have to be pointed out by an interpretation board, a leaflet or a website. Having grasped the basic concept it is then quite difficult to work out where the Waterline goes on the map, or the difference between the ages of its various parts.

When walking or cycling around (driving is too fast) one does eventually develop the ability to identify possible Waterline features, but sometimes they turn out to be just an 'ordinary' dyke or canal. The Waterline was a defensive structure, relying not on a physical presence, such as England's Hadrian's Wall or the Great Wall of China, but a kind of absence, a threat rather than an action, causing fear, uncertainty and confusion rather than outright confrontation.

The Waterline was essentially a line of defences around the core of the country: the provinces of North and South Holland and some neighbouring territory, which relied mostly on the opportunity to deliberately flood the countryside to a depth of about 40 cm (16 in), deep enough to slow down or stop horses, carts and vehicles, but not deep enough to enable boats of any size to sail effectively. The concealment of ditches and canals (or more recently barbed wire or mines) made the water body even more intimidating. The idea came from the desperate improvised flooding of the countryside during the Dutch Revolt against Spain of 1568–1648 when several attempts at besieging cities by the Spanish were foiled. From then on, the system had a patchy record: it worked against an attempted French invasion in 1672, but failed when the French invaded again in the winter of 1794–5 and the water froze. On other occasions the water was not released in time and in 1940 technology in the form of air power enabled Nazi Germany to circumvent its effectiveness. But then the Great Wall of China did not have a better record, as Chinese history relates.

The Waterline basically consisted of a series of dykes arranged so that the water on the side of possible enemies, essentially east and south, could be flooded. The first version was started in 1629; the 'Old Waterline' stretched down from Naarden on the (former) Zuiderzee, east of Amsterdam down to the Biesbosch, the marshiness of which was as good a natural defence as any. However, a bulge left the city of Utrecht unprotected, so in 1815, a new Waterline was started which went east of this key city. Today, all surviving parts are recorded, with cycleways and footpaths enabling both lines to be traced, and all the forts and other structures along the routes visited. Each line comprised a range of different elements, including several distinct subsidiary 'lines' which always featured a dyke and an associated military road and often a canal. At the 'top end' near Vecht, there is a museum with maps and artefacts and a huge waterfilled model to explain the occasionally bewildering nature of the project.

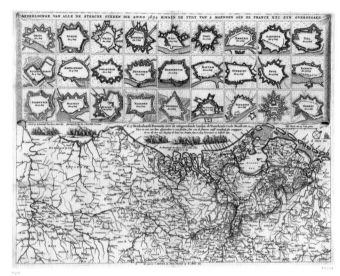

01

02

03

Strategic points were covered by forts and it is these forts that are the main feature of the Waterline today. In cycling along a dyke visitors believe they are 'on' the Waterline because the guidebook tells them so, whereas a fort rears up in the countryside so dramatically that even the speeding motorist will see it.

The fortifications of the Waterline introduce into the landscape elements normally lacking here: miniature and rather dramatic hills, slopes, ravines and vistas, and with the increasing tree growth on many of them over time, a sense of enclosure and mystery, even intimacy.

The engineered battlements and revetments are similar to those of the more modern dykes but are somehow tighter and more severe, further enhancing the impression that the whole landscape could have been shaped by directions from a drawing board.

There are some particularly impressive fortress towns too, which first manifest themselves as canals obstructing access from one part of town to another, or which offer picturesque views across water bodies to tree-lined avenues. Actually visualizing them however requires a map, an aerial photograph or Google Earth; a bit like the famous lines on the desert in Nazca in Peru, the fortifications of the Waterline hide their ability to astonish those who are earth-bound. Such concealment, the incapacity of that part of our brain to make a mental map of these surroundings, must have been part of their defensive capacity too. Invading troops would not know what to make of what was in front of them, for part of the idea of a star fort is that it keeps the enemy guessing – it is impossible to face the defenders head-on, and there is always the fear of a cannon ball or bullet coming in from the side or even behind you.

Forts and castles normally impose themselves on the countryside with stone or, latterly, cement, but this being The Netherlands several centuries ago, neither was available in much quantity, so earth was used instead. In doing so, French military technology was employed, and hereby hangs an interesting point. During the 17th and 18th centuries, the French were the dominant military power in Europe and the most technologically advanced. Their use of earthworks to create defensive positions, using the spades of their armies, or recruited men, was a breakthrough in military engineering. The court of Louis XIV also then found another use for the army engineers, their pattern books and men: embankments, lakes and terraces in gardens. The link between

04

05

06

07

01
A map of 1672 showing the outline of the Waterline and its fortresses.

02
Washland in the landscape.

03
Fort Nigtevecht, part of the Dutch Waterline.

04
The 17th-century defence fortifications of Naarden, restored in 1970.

05
A fortification north of Spaarndam, part of the 'Stelling of Amsterdam', a defence ring around the city of Amsterdam at 15–20 km (8–12 miles) from the centre.

06
The French siege of Bergen op Zoom, 16 July 1747.

07
The vicious thorns of blackthorn (Prunus spinosa) are an excellent natural anti-personnel weapon

military and landscape engineering is direct and immediate. Water, needless to say, played a crucial role in The Netherlands, with canals backed by embankments being the basic defensive combination.

There was even a defensive role for plants. The rapid growth of trees and shrubs would help to camouflage the forts so that they would look like innocent hills to an invading army. Any attempt to climb the hills would result in getting tangled up with the final Dutch secret weapons, hawthorn (Crataegus persimilis) and blackthorn (Prunus spinosa), whose 4-cm (1½-in) long thorns still puncture thousands of car tyres a year in the UK when country hedges are cut every summer. The vicious spines can penetrate deeply and quite frequently cause painful long-term infections, and the shrub suckers very vigorously. A better design for an ideal defensive plant could not be wished for.

With time and the invention of cement the fortresses acquired walls, bunkers, storerooms, barracks, stronger emplacements for guns, and all the facilities needed by the modernized warfare of the early 20th century. In the end, though, the Waterline was useless against the worst human enemy the Dutch had had to face since the Spanish, and while there was some theoretical use of it against the Russian invasion that Cold War politicians and military planners expected during the 1950s and 1960s, the concept was eventually quietly dropped. In an age of potential nuclear warfare, it began to seem pointless.

The forts, too big and expensive to demolish, mouldered away for the rest of the 20th century. Trees grew and the forts often became ideal places for wildlife, away from people and the increasingly intensely managed countryside. They also became wonderful places for children to play, full of secret paths, places to build dens, and mysterious structures such as vast doors or gunports to feed the imagination (and no doubt many youthful fears). For many children they would have been the first and perhaps the only experience of rising ground and places where a good view of the surrounding countryside could be had.

Today, the forts have been rediscovered as heritage. A number of them have been converted into homes, exhibition centres, restaurants, and of course museums, while the ecological value of many has been recognized too.

Vis
à
Vis

Sustainability may be the buzzword of our time, but as a concept it does encapsulate issues that are fundamental to our continued survival and that of all other living things on planet Earth. For a long time the garden design and landscape industry as a whole has been no better than any other industry at the development of sustainable practices. However, there has always been a minority of individuals who have been really committed to working in a more sustainable way, which, given the subject matter of plants and the environment, is not surprising. They have acted as a vanguard for ideas, a testing ground for materials and practices and a showpiece for successful schemes. Thanks to them, the industry as a whole is now mending its ways, and is set to play an increasingly important role in developing environments that do not just stop things getting worse but actually play a positive role. Green roofs, sustainable urban drainage schemes and urban forestry are among the measures that are part of this relatively new field of environmental amelioration.

Vis à Vis have been making and designing private gardens as well as landscapes for institutions, schools, companies and local municipalities since 1994. 'From the start,' says Margo van Beem, 'we made the choice to work only with sustainable materials. This was not always the easiest route – the unfamiliarity of some of the materials, their poor availability and sometimes their quality were obstacles that we had to overcome in the beginning.' Now that the movement for sustainability is growing, particularly among young people, finding quality materials has become very much easier, with a growing expectation from clients, and from government bodies, that sustainability is put right at the centre of the garden and landscaping business.

The ultimate act of recycling in this context of course is that of reusing a building or other structure. This is the case with the garden Margo and her business partner Emiel Versluis made for a client who had an apartment in an old Waterline fortress.

Wooden decking and chunky lush moisture-loving plants integrate the garden with the canal that runs alongside. Smaller perennials weave between the larger ones, for this is habitat planting that aims at filling all available space with life. Water inevitably features in many Dutch gardens, but the sustainability ethos does not just regard it as something to be simply enjoyed, rather it aims at directing, managing and channelling it in ways that reduce flooding and slow its passage through the environment. Gardens may feature green roofs on structures to reduce runoff, with systems to capture what does drain off for later use. The concept of the natural swimming pool is of course embraced, the perfect way to combine function with naturalistic wetland planting. The planted area of a natural swimming pool is the bit which carries out the filtration and cleaning work, and with its domination by the firmly linear foliage of waterside plants, visually it can very effectively blur the distinction between waterside and planted border.

Some sustainable garden features do have an aesthetic which challenges conventional notions of garden tidiness, such as paving blocks which incorporate small patches of soil in which grass can grow, creating an effect which being neither hard surface nor lawn challenges those who like their categories hard and fast. They act as an effective porous pavement, allowing water to soak away into the ground. Another is the log wall, an excellent high-density wildlife habitat which, when it ages, can look too far along the road of decay for some tastes.

01
Varieties of *Hosta* and
Rodgersia join traditional
pollarded willows.

01

02

03

04

There is also some radical thinking on the subject of materials, which is very refreshing to hear. 'We try to use as few materials as possible,' says Margo, 'and we think about the lifespan of projects, asking how long something really needs to last, if it is for example a small urban garden.'

The implication is that such gardens are, realistically, highly likely to be remodelled after a certain number of years, so constructing with timber that lasts for a very long time is likely to be wasteful and shorter-lifespan softwood is in fact more appropriate. This is in contrast to those so-called green projects that use oak or teak, which however sustainably grown will be taken apart and possibly disposed of in a few years' time when another home owner decides on a make-over.

Where more long-lived materials are needed, alternatives to unsustainably-harvested hardwoods have increasingly become available. Margo recommends robinia as an alternative to tropical hardwoods, European-grown Douglas fir and chestnut, and Accoya®, the last being *Pinus radiata* timber which is treated with acetic acid to produce an extremely durable timber. Ersatz timber made from recycled plastic can look remarkably like the real thing while being extremely durable.

02
A rill combined with decking.

03
Hosta 'Big Daddy' and *Rodgersia aesculifolia*.

04
Paving interspersed with vegetation can improve drainage.

05

06

07

08

09

05
A stepped water feature.

06
A pergola leading to
a conservatory.

07
Himalayan 'candelabra'
varieties of *Primula*.

08
Elegant and innovative
detailing on the decking.

09
A seating area
cantilevered over
the water.

Emiel says that he is the architect and designer, while Margo is his plantswoman: 'I think about what atmosphere the garden should have, I draw the big lines and she does the technical details and the planting – and the planting is now our strongest selling point.'

01

02

Margo and Emiel met when they worked for Ruurd van Donkelaar at his small specialist garden centre, initially doing Saturday and holiday jobs while at a horticultural college. Recognizing their talent for drawing and love of plants, Ruurd took them to other nurseries and on trips to botanic and other public gardens, including the German experimental gardens Sichtungsgarten Weihenstephan near Munich and Sichtungsgarten Hermannshof in Weinheim. Eventually they even went into business together for a number of years with a design studio, although Ruurd left the business in 2004.

'We called it Vis à Vis (Face to Face) because we wanted to stress the direct relationship with the client,' explains Margo. 'Gardens at the time were very architectural and with little scope for ecology,' adds Emiel, 'or they were very English-Romantic inspired. I had had an education at an art academy so I wanted something more contemporary. I was excited by modern materials like corten steel and galvanized metal, combined with naturalistic plants in a bold style.'

Describing these early years, Emiel recalls 'going to shows where we would have a stand like a garden table where all the dishes were small maquettes of garden designs we had made, or a mock-up of an outhouse where you could peek through the hedge holes to see if the neighbour's garden was greener than yours . . . everybody who saw it left us with a smile, instead of all those grumpy faces you normally see on this events.'

Emiel says that he is the architect and designer, while Margo is his plantswoman: 'I think about what atmosphere the garden should have, I draw the big lines and she does the technical details and the planting – and the planting is now our strongest selling point.' He describes how he worked a lot with architects and so looked to architecture and art, wanting to do something different with garden design. 'Mien Ruys is not important for me. I was more inspired by trips to Parc Citroën, a very significant park designed by a number of architects and the leading French planting designer Gilles Clément, with its combination of big plan and the small pocket gardens; Museum Insel Holmbroich, an enigmatic art museum/ installation in North Rhine-Westphalia, Germany, with its inside-and-outside experience; post-industrial projects in the

German Ruhrgebiet (the old industrial region); Sichtungsgarten Hermannshof, the leading example of contemporary German planting design; and the now well-known garden show at Chaumont-sur-Loire.'

Their firmly contemporary list of inspiration marks Vis à Vis out as practitioners more in line with landscape architects than garden designers. 'I have however learnt a lot about plants,' Emiel says, 'and our designs now are focused on the plants, but we have no favourites, as I think it is important to look at the whole and not at particular species. We learnt to look at natural vegetation and relate it to gardens, and to use plants in a more naturalistic way, like the Hansen and Stahl book *Die Stauden und ihre Lebensbereiche.*'

Margo's early influences included books by Elisabeth de Lestrieux, an extraordinarily prolific writer of 36 gardening books in the last quarter of the 20th century whose style of choice was very much English Romantic, and Henk Gerritsen, whose gardening experience at the Priona Gardens were disseminated through his book collaborations with his partner, the photographer Anton Schlepers, and Piet Oudolf, and later, a book of his own, *Essay on Gardening* (2014). His approach was heavily orientated to wild flowers and the application of elementary

03

04

plant ecological science to garden plantings. For Margo and Emiel, his approach, and that of Ruurd van Donkelaar, is far more appropriate to the current situation than that of Piet Oudolf, as they stress the interrelationships of plants and their relationship to fauna – they feel that they are far more authentic ecologically. They like to use native plants where this is possible and appropriate, but in a typical spirit of pragmatism recognize that this is not always desirable, in small gardens for instance, where aesthetics are important. The range of wild plants from commercial nurseries has also often been restricted, although now this availability seems to be on the increase again.

01
White deadnettle
(*Lamium album*).

02
Cardoon (*Cynara
cardunculus*).

03
Purple loosestrife (*Lythrum
salicaria* 'Blush').

04
Siberian purslane (*Montia
sibirica*), which is edible.

05
Wild flowers of the
woodland edge.

05

01

01
The filtration strip of a natural swimming pool.

02
Sending rainwater into a garden wetland.

03
A wooden wall invertebrate habitat.

04
Paving designed to green over.

02

03

04

05

05
The amount of greenery that thrives depends on the level of foot traffic.

06
A corner of an ornamental wetland.

07
Purple loosestrife (*Lythrum salicaria*) flowers for months in summer.

08
Clean, bio-filtered water!

06

07

08

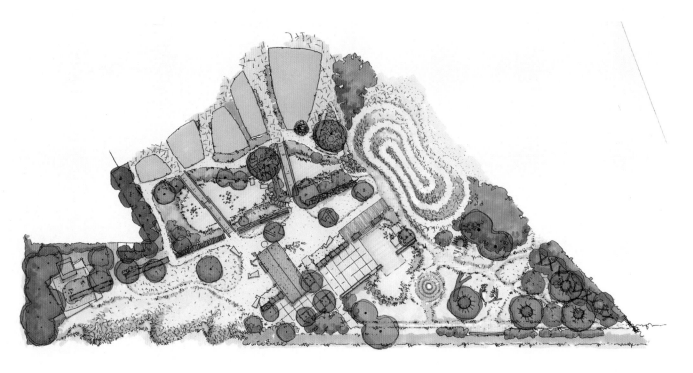

01

The jewel in the crown of Emiel and Margo's work is the 0.5 hectare (1¼ acre) garden they planned and built for De Wilde Weelde Wereld at Appeltern.

01
The plan for the garden at Wilde Weelde Wereld.

02
A boardwalk ramp.

03
Walls of recycled paving.

04
Verbena bonariensis, a very good butterfly plant.

05
Annual wild flowers in a multi-habitat space.

06
Caltha palustris, a wetland or marginal spring wild flower.

De Wilde Weelde is a trade association of companies that aim to work as sustainably as possible throughout The Netherlands. The Wereld (world) project is part of the Gardens of Appeltern, which bring together a large number of show gardens with the aim of inspiring private gardeners; it brands itself as a 'garden ideas park'. De Wilde Weelde itself is a project organized by the Oase Foundation, a body which since 1993 has promoted sustainable and wildlife-friendly gardening, with a big focus on community projects and education.

The Vis à Vis garden at De Wilde Weelde Wereld centres on a natural swimming pool with some dramatic walls and terraces built of reused bricks and other materials. The project is by no means aimed only at private gardeners, for a very strong part of the ecological garden movement in The Netherlands has always been geared towards institutional users such as schools and community associations. The maintenance of these places is in the hands of either professionals or volunteers, all of whom are able to benefit from the very impressive Oase Foundation education programme.

For private gardeners, however, Vis à Vis offers an interesting service – garden coaching. This practice, somewhere between employing a designer and having a gardener, is well established in the USA but is little known in Europe. The owner of the newly installed Vis à Vis garden is talked through what they have, usually by Margo, with a series of training sessions. 'We can work together to prune, transplant, mulch, and so forth,' says Margo. 'Gardeners learn to recognize what is a part of the garden and what weeds need to be removed, and we can advise them to experiment with annual and biennial plants, bulbs, vegetables or other plants.' There is even the possibility of a manual being drawn up especially for the new garden owner. 'It's a relationship that works both ways,' Margo says, 'as it helps people to learn and take pleasure in the garden while the designer can keep an eye on its development and encourage the owner to guide it in the right direction.'

A love of contemporary materials and design does not usually go with naturalistic planting, but Vis à Vis are showing that this is potentially a powerful and effective combination, especially when combined with an approach that is principled in its use of sustainable resources.

02

03

05

04

06

'God made the world, but the Dutch made Holland.'

One of the things that strikes the visitor almost anywhere in The Netherlands is the sheer artificiality of much of the landscape. There are so many straight lines, and everything is so neat: trees regularly spaced along roads, embankments wending their way for miles across the landscape at exactly the same gradient and huge, entirely level fields with plough furrows all precisely the same height. Canals cut straight as an arrow as far as you can see (or at least as far as the next bridge), and it is clear, even from a distance, that every tree in the blocks of woodland has been planted on a grid.

True, this is more so in some areas than others. In those with a longer history of settlement, fields are smaller and more irregular, dykes are more likely to curve, or be uneven; there are more surprises, and it is often clear that there have been many centuries of piecemeal digging, planting and embanking. The most recently reclaimed areas can feel almost disconcertingly artificial: huge fields, no curves or bends, a uniformity that can be seen almost nowhere else on earth.

The disparity between old and new landscapes shows us that the monumental scale of the new ones took a lot of practice. Today's gently sloping dyke abutting the drainage ditch that maintains its width for what seems like miles, before turning abruptly into shiny ryegrass for what feels like eternity, is the result of near on a thousand years of experimentation: of digging, pile-driving, seaweed harvesting, brushwood weaving, wheelbarrowing, baling out, tree pruning, thatching, sawing,

and all the other myriad operations that make a landscape. The geometry and efficiency of the modern landscape is the sum total of millions of days of human experience, much of it gained while being very wet, very cold, very tired, and sometimes, utterly desperate.

Flying above the landscape is perhaps the best way to appreciate it, an experience that will be limited to arriving or leaving Schiphol Airport for most of us. Google Earth of course can give us a virtual representation. Maps do not have the drama but can clarify. Drones and church towers offer a dramatic but more oblique plan-view. With these aerial views, perhaps more than anywhere else, is it possible to appreciate the meaning of the saying that 'God made the world, but the Dutch made Holland'.

When you travel around the modern Dutch landscape, especially somewhere like Flevoland (finished c.1968), there are times when you may appreciate it as very

beautiful, in an abstract kind of a way: the evenness, the repetition of forms, the flat play of light. Surface textures may be created by rows of crops, harvested potatoes awaiting scooping up, or ground obviously shaped by machinery. After a while any irregularity becomes welcome: wild flowers in a ditch, a slight kink in a canal, an irregular fuzz of trees on the horizon. Though these truly engineered landscapes may enable the efficient keeping back of the waters, incredible levels of food production and straight roads, to many visitors – and to increasing numbers of Dutch people over the years – they have also been alienating, and the old world of fields dotted with wild flowers and bendy canals with old willow pollards leaning over them seem more homely and more attractive.

The core to all this intense land management is defending existing land, much of it below sea level, from inundation. To this end all else is subservient.

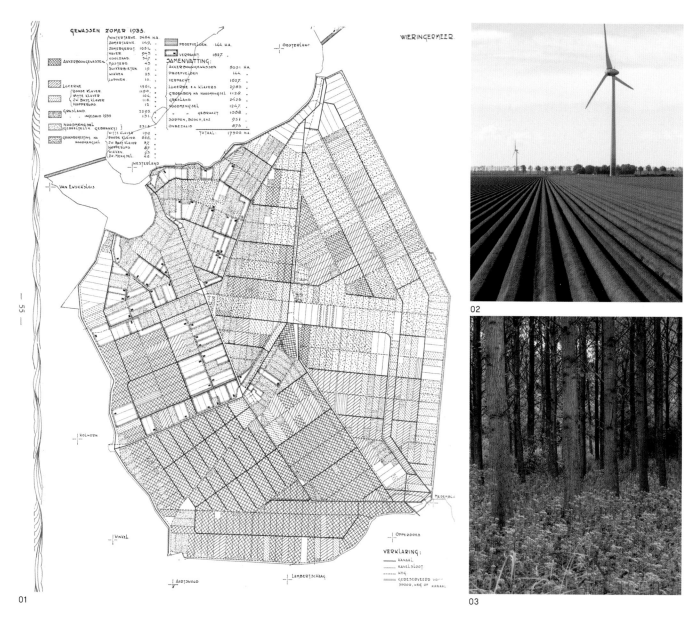

01

02

03

Historically this has meant that navigable rivers and canals have had to take shipping on circuitous routes, in particular avoiding any breaches in the defensive line of sand dunes along the coast. If this has meant laboriously transhipping goods, so be it. This was necessary when a ship on a canal could not get to water on another level, and everything on it had to be taken off – usually literally manhandled off and onto another ship on the other level. This would often be needed at a dam, which has given us place names such as Rotterdam and Amsterdam; at the latter, transhipped goods came on or off ships waiting at quays on the Zuiderzee, before or after their roundabout route to the North Sea. The key to keeping water back lies with the polder, an area of land surrounded by dykes, so that its level is lower than the land around

it. Within the polder there are usually many canals and drainage ditches which draw water off the land so it can then be pumped out, formerly by windmills, then steam and then diesel or electric pumps. The first polders must have been tiny, dug out by hand in the medieval period. Over time they have got larger, and their lines straighter. Older polders are more likely to be crossed with multiple small drainage canals; the older the landscape, the more detail and the more intricate the channelling. Polders of the 20th century can be so vast, enclosing so much ground, that it is difficult to read them as such. So crucial are polders that the term 'polder landscape' is used to describe them.

Many polders were created by digging a channel around a lake or area of wet ground, forming a ring (with a ring-

dyke on the outside), and pumping water out of it until the level in the new polder sank enough to leave the land dry enough to be usable. It could then have drainage canals cut across it to further dry it out. Sometimes internal dykes were created, so that if the outer dyke broke, not all of the polder would be lost. Creating polders required co-operation between landowners, neighbouring communities and those who lived downstream of any increased water flow as the polder was dried out. This co-operation became hard-wired into the country's political culture over time; by the 1990s there was even a term 'polder model', used to describe consensus politics and a pragmatic acceptance of differences.

While polder landscapes often represented taking the offensive against the waters, claiming them for human use,

04

05

06

07

08

09

the country's river landscapes were more defensive. Much of The Netherlands was flood plain, with the rivers able to expand across the landscape during wet periods. As dykes rose in the development of polder landscapes, the flood plains became more constrained, forcing the rivers into ever narrower channels; during floods they would deposit sand and mud on their outer slower reaches, so that as the water fell it left banks behind (known as levées) and the riverbed itself at a higher level, potentially dangerous for local communities on the other side of the bank the next time there was a flood. Inevitably river control and management became as crucial for many communities as polder creation was for others.

The world over, the management of rivers in flood concentrated on control and embankment, and very often straightening. The latter part of the 20th century saw greater pragmatism, as water engineers began to appreciate that the natural meanders of a river can hold more flood water than artificially straightened ones, and that marshlands can be valuable emergency reservoirs for water. The early 2000s saw the development of 'Space for the River', a programme that combined raising and strengthening dykes with the creation of areas that the river could expand into during floods, in some cases sacrificing farms and land hard-won from the waters by previous generations. Some of these new zones have been made into nature reserves, an example perhaps of water engineering coming full circle, embracing natural environments as a tool and a necessity.

01
The cropping plan for the first year (1935) of the Wieringermeer.

02
Wind turbine and ploughed field, Flevoland.

03
Poplars, regularly spaced.

04
The Van Starkenborgh canal.

05
A field of mangold.

06
A harvested field behind a dyke.

07
Potatoes waiting to be collected.

08
The orderliness of a polder landscape.

09
The vanishing point, Flevopolder.

INSPIRED BY CULTURAL LANDSCAPES

Donders! & van der Heiden

'The whole of Holland is like a private garden,' says Pierre van der Heiden. 'The entire landscape is organized on a rational basis, everything has been designed, and indeed designed several times; all the nature is artificial. At college you are taught on landscape courses that everything can be designed and shaped the way you want it, which in one sense is wonderful.' Pierre, like many people here, is ambivalent, adding 'After World War II there was a process of rationalization and consolidation. It changed the landscape enormously and made us a wealthy country, but because of that Holland has become a product, and biodiversity has been lost.' In talking about private gardens, it is clear that he sees them partly as a refuge, a space in which to get a better sense of balance.

The partnership of Donders! & van der Heiden is nothing if not prolific. Their website lists a great number of projects of all sizes, from small town gardens to substantial rural ones. A visit to them to see some of their gardens in the region packs in a lot too – even walking through the streets of the couple's home town of Apeldoorn can be a namecheck of projects, as Monique Donders casually recalls 'We did that one over there – you can peer over the hedge if you like.'

Their style is for modernist clean lines and simple graphic blocks of clipped shrubs – often box or yew, and often quite long. Many of their gardens could be described as minimalist, for clients who like everything simple and don't actually want to do much gardening. There is more than a hint of the highly organized and rational Dutch agricultural landscape. Some surprises can come with changes of level, notable in a flat landscape, including paving higher than areas of ground cover, such as periwinkle (*Vinca* spp.). The planting cannot

be walked on, so the psychological effect is of walking along next to water.

Some gardens feature perennials, usually in the same rectangular blocks that the clipped box or yew take – big, uninhibited borders of perennials, making a strong contrast with the straight lines and restraint of the rest of the garden. Some perennial plantings can be quite minimalist, though, as with one town garden where a long line of *Persicaria amplexicaulis* makes a real statement in late summer. It is combined with just a few other species for interest earlier in the season.

Monique Donders and Pierre van der Heiden are a couple who have known each other for more than 30 years, and have been in business together for around half that time. Their closeness helps to explain something about their design practice that most people find extraordinary. Pierre, who has elements of autism, almost never meets clients or visits the site; Monique is the public face of the business. 'She is the eyes and ears,' Pierre says. 'She

gets the information we need from clients and filters it, relaying it to me – she takes videos, too. When she works with couples they both have to be present during discussions about their garden. I pick up her feelings, my antennae work overtime . . . we know each other so well. It's a risk, but it keeps me sharp. Doing it this way, I don't get the noise, I get only the facts from Monique – she focuses on what's important.' In developing a design, Pierre says, 'I have to imagine going into that space with my eyes shut, opening them, turning around through 360 degrees and closing them again. The impression in the mind is a certain feeling of the place – we refer to that as its essence and that's what I'm looking for. Every single place, whether beautiful or ugly, leaves a certain emotion behind and that is important – it does not matter if the essence is good or bad, but when I feel I have it, that's the moment to have a new conversation with Monique, to make sure that we agree on it. Then I am on my own, designing the garden.'

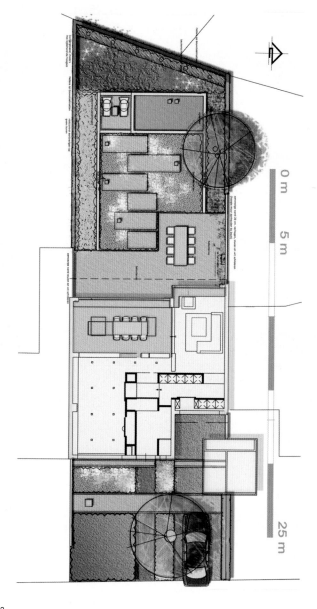

01

02

01
Garden minimalism.

02
The plan for a small
town garden.

Describing in detail his design process, Pierre says, 'In the early days I would start on a design and feel I had so many possibilities, like a house with ten doors – you open a door and then there are another ten doors and so you have something like a tree with endlessly branching possibilities. Now I feel much more confident when I am on the right track, and when I am not, I can go backwards to the point at which another decision might need to be made. Being able to go back and reconsider then move forward on another track is a big difference with my work earlier in my career.'

Once he has made a design he discusses it with Monique: 'We have to agree totally on the end result, though sometimes this is a fight. When we present it to the customer, it's a possibility, and we'll work as long as necessary to get it right for them. We never do options – we present in detail with plans, 3D perspectives, and whatever else might be needed.' Monique adds, 'Sometimes we have to explain to the clients what we are proposing as they don't always get it right away. We need to explore their limits – some get scared easily!'

The secret of the couple's success with what many in the profession, or indeed out of it, might find an odd way of working is that gardens have always been a central part of their long relationship. 'We are complementary and interdependent – we could not do this individually,' says Pierre.

03
Concrete slabs in three sizes.

04
The slabs appear to float on a sea of periwinkle (*Vinca minor*).

05
The bamboo *Fargesia* 'Jiuzhaigou'.

03

04

05

GARDENS UNDER BIG SKIES

01

INSPIRED BY CULTURAL LANDSCAPES

02

03

04

05

'When we were young we travelled around Europe a lot, visiting gardens. We'd arrive on a motorbike, and people sometimes found our youth and biking leathers surprising in that context.' He lists as particular sources of inspiration Villa Gamberaia near Florence, Villa Ephrussi de Rothschild at St-Jean-Cap-Ferrat in France, and the Chelsea Flower Show.

There is no doubting Pierre's strong visual imagination. 'When I design a garden,' he says, 'I have a picture of it five years later in my head, so I can find it hard when a client is enthusiastic about a new garden. I think 'call me a couple of years later and be enthusiastic then', Monique adding, 'I can see through a young garden.' Organization is crucial. 'I manage the contractors,' says Monique. 'We know who to go to for what – it is quite formulaic.' She uses a group app on a mobile phone to co-ordinate them, which is a very effective way of keeping everyone informed, including the clients – though Pierre chooses not to be a part of this.

The couple have often collaborated with planting consultants but now work exclusively with Ruurd van Donkelaar, who not only produces planting plans but also creates a book for each client. This is a personalized manual with pictures of the plants, information about them, care and maintenance instructions, biodiversity information, and their country of origin. 'It's a way for clients to learn and encourages them to love the garden and its plants, and to communicate that to their family.' He is brought in when the design is finished, and there are discussions with the client on what kind of planting they want and the level of maintenance they are happy with. 'I write down "low maintenance" and "privacy" almost every time,' he says. 'I have to understand the possibilities of the site to help decide the feeling that the planting will create. Pierre designs the spaces, I fill them in.'

01
(See p.166)
Echinacea purpurea
'Pica Bella', *Origanum*
'Rosenkuppel' and
Verbena bonariensis.

02
(See p.167) *Echinacea*
pallida.

03
Echinacea purpurea and
pale blue *Salvia yangii*
colour a border
in midsummer.

04
Cool expanses of grass
contrast with the colourful
borders.

05
Echinacea pallida
dominates this stretch
of border.

06
From midsummer,
seedheads become
increasingly important
visually.

07
Borders alternating
with lawns.

06

07

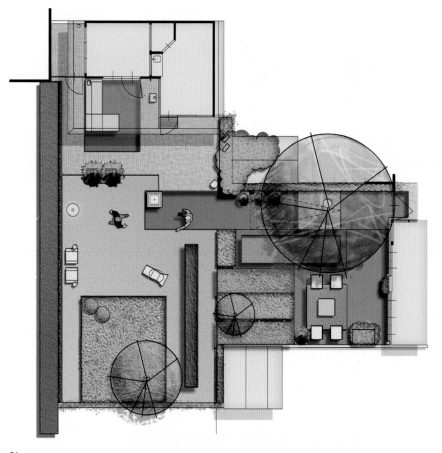

01

Ruurd uses a concept developed by Richard Hansen and Friedrich Stahl, two German researchers who compiled a whole series of planting combinations organized by both habitat and level of maintenance. Their system enabled a great many landscape and garden designers in Germany to create complex plantings, but since it was originally developed for the continental climate of Bavaria, Ruurd has adapted it for the more forgiving climate of The Netherlands. 'Sometimes I design plantings in groups,' he says, 'sometimes mixed, intermingled combinations, sometimes in layers. Ninety per cent of the plants I use are reliable, but I like at least 10 per cent adventure.' This means plants he is less familiar with, or those that are not predictable.

'I like the clear lines of Holland,' says Pierre. 'They give me a sense of clarity in my mind.' These clear lines are obviously reflected in the partnership's work, but, he says, 'Having Ruurd involved is important, because straight lines are simple and restful but only through planting can you see the seasons and appreciate change and decay. His planting softens the hardness of lines.' In recent commissions, perennials seem to be breaking out even more, beating back the hard lines and chunky graphics of grasses and clipped shrubs; some gardens now involve quite extensive areas of perennials with diverse mixes of species.

In creating a balance between the graphic strength of lines and the natural chaos of vegetation, Donders! & van der Heiden are perhaps mapping a microcosm of the creative tension between the nation's attitude to its engineered landscape and a yearning for something of a freer and more unregulated nature.

01
The plan of Monique and Pierre's private garden.

02
Strong foliage shapes are a feature here.

03
Blocks of hedging contrast with softer perennial forms.

02

03

01
Balls of *Enkianthus campanulatus* turn fiery red in autumn.

02
White lines bringing elements together.

03
The softness of mixed herbaceous planting contrasts with the many graphic forms of this garden.

01

02

03

INSPIRED BY CULTURAL LANDSCAPES

04

05

06

04
This is primarily a garden
of geometrical shapes.

05
Ferns and perennial
foliage contrast with
hard lines.

06
Aristolochia macrophylla
is one of the best hardy
foliage climbers.

INSPIRED BY LANDSCAPE DESIGNERS

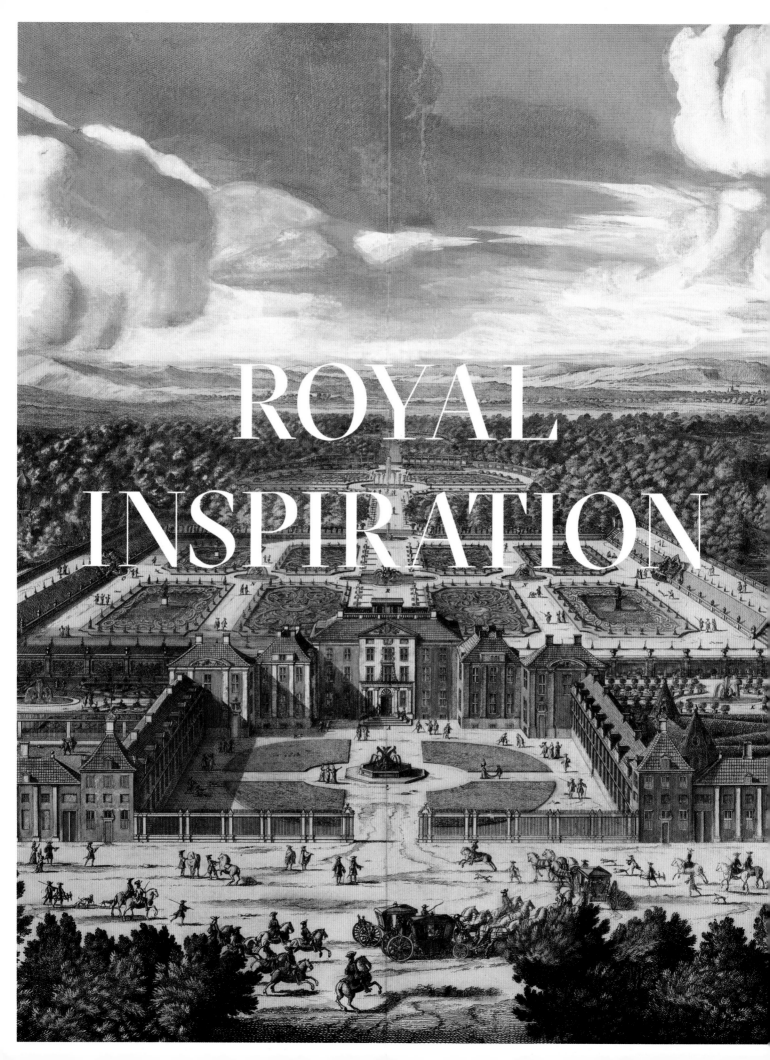

ROYAL
INSPIRATION

Het Loo is one of those Baroque gardens that today feels like a throwback to a far-distant age, one where vegetation was treated as a material as plastic as clay, and where the labour to maintain it in a profoundly unnatural form was cheap. Designed to impress, and impose itself on visitors of distinction and those few members of the citizenry who might have gained a glimpse, it speaks of an age when making a garden was not just an art form but also a way of conveying messages of power, authority and wealth.

Laid out by Stadtholder William III (who was also William III of England) and his consort Mary between 1684 and 1686, it was designed by Claude Desgots (c.1658–1732). Desgots was a French architect and landscape designer, a pupil and follower of André Le Nôtre, the designer of the gardens at Vaux-le-Vicomte and Versailles that established the pattern for gardens in France up to the Revolution, and indeed beyond, in terms of both time and place. Versailles and French Baroque gardens generally were reflections of an autocratic monarchy and a confident and overbearing aristocracy, their sight lines stretching to the far horizon, implying that it was not just the garden that belonged to the owner but everything else visible too. A Dutch Stadtholder was different, and Het Loo's garden reflects this. Although effectively a hereditary post, 'Stadtholder' implies a less monarchical approach to rule than 'King', one more dependent on the agreement of the country's provinces (the national taste for compromise perhaps).

Het Loo's garden does not seek total domination of its surroundings; instead it is more inward-looking, surrounded by trees, and with a raised walkway all around the perimeter, so that anyone walking along it will be looking inwards, and, crucially, downwards.

Nevertheless, the full glory of the ornate parterres set among beds of coloured gravel would only have been visible to those in the upper rooms of the palace, a privileged position (although the numerous servants would have had this view too). The 'view from above' is something that is very important in urban Dutch gardens, with houses traditionally being narrow and tall, so gardens would be more likely to be seen from above than at ground level. This must have been one of the many factors that helped the popularity of patterns made with box hedges.

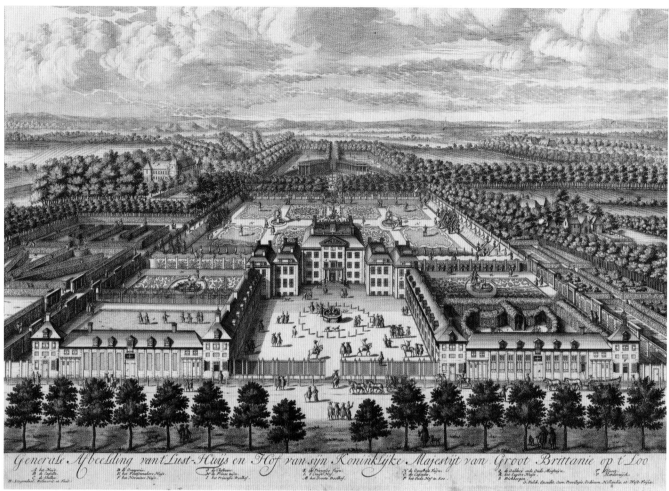

Generale Afbeelding van 't Lust-Huys en Hof van sijn Koninklijke Majestijt van Groot Brittanie op 't Loo

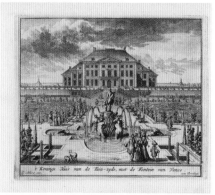

De Koninginne Tuin met 't Groene Kabinet; en de Oranjerie, van Achteren te zien

INSPIRED BY LANDSCAPE DESIGNERS

05

01
A general view of Het Loo.

02
The gate on the road
leading to Apeldoorn.

03
An 18th-century print of
the Fountain of Venus.

04
The 'green cabinet' –
trelliswork with beech
trained over it.

05
Portrait of Prince
William and Maria-
Henriette Stuart.

At ground level, the patterns of the parterre at Het Loo would be difficult to make out. Interest is focused more on the statuary, an essential status symbol in any royal or aristocratic garden of the time. Narrow borders of flowering plants are also a source of interest when walking the paths. Today their contents, mostly annuals, are considered unremarkable by most visitors, unless particularly artfully arranged. In the past, however, this would have been like an exhibition space for showing off new plant introductions and rarities; as with everything else here, this was a means of showing off the wealth, status and good taste of the ruling family.

Few of the ornate formal gardens of this period survive anywhere in Europe. True, they went out of fashion as the 'English landscape style' swept over the continent, but more fundamentally, they deteriorated; being so labour-intensive, there would have been pressure to cut costs and simplify the planting.

Once it is no longer pristine, the dense pattern of clipped box and yew loses crispness as well as status and so the landscape parkland style, with a few strategic trees among acres of grass mown by grazing livestock, then becomes a temptingly cheap alternative. Over the course of the 18th century, Het Loo's Baroque garden was replaced with this kind of landscape in a series of stages.

The first, at some point early in the century, was the development of an outer zone that was more park than garden, a transition to the world beyond the royal or aristocratic domain. This was in common with many of the other great European formal gardens of this period. Here mature trees, grass and occasional water bodies made for a simple, cool, restrained environment, far more relaxed than the highly orchestrated knots of the formal parterres. Canals could be straight, or they could curve, or they could expand into lakes, and in doing so lose the last touches of formality. Whatever they did, they showed that a less obviously dictatorial way of ordering nature was possible within the royal domain. As time went on, the style of these more relaxed outer areas crept inwards, replacing the parterres and gravel, partly for the simple reason that they were cheaper to maintain, as well as being better suited to the ethos of the times which increasingly reacted against garden formality.

After the death of the last Dutch royal to live at Het Loo, in 1962, the palace and garden became a national museum and the intention was expressed to restore the landscape, although this did not start in earnest until 1975, when a research process was begun to look at maps and documents from the time of the garden's heyday. Restoration itself has been a slow process, with the main phase being completed between 2007 and 2015. Today it is possible to see something that is pretty close to how the garden was in the time of William and Mary.

Looking at the big picture, it is really only the scale and ambition of Het Loo which is unusual to us today; many of its features are endlessly repeated in domestic gardens up and down the country. In fact it would not be too wide of the mark to say that the Baroque look has been the most influential garden style in the Netherlands ever: pleached limes, box bushes clipped into geometric shapes, both as individuals (often cones or balls) or collectively as dwarf hedges defining squares, circles or more complex forms. These may be miniature or very attenuated versions of Het Loo's magnificence, but their ubiquity is a sign of a deep and widespread love for garden formality; far more so than in neighbouring countries, even in France, homeland of the style.

One reason for the popularity of the formal garden style is that it is a way of making sense of a flat landscape. Views are dependent on elevation, and where there is no elevation, it is physically difficult to see much of the garden once a few trees and shrubs have grown.

Giving order and sense to space on a flat plot involves creating sight lines, and the classical tradition is a very good way of doing this. The story of gardening is very much one of 'top down' – what the king did was copied by the court and the aristocracy, which was copied by the gentry and then by anyone who had the space and the means to create an ornamental garden. So, it is no surprise that the French-style garden commissioned by William III soon inspired imitations reaching all the way through the social hierarchy. By the time the style reached the tiny yards of artisans there was no question of making sense of open landscapes, of course; instead the style spelled intention, creativity and skill, and gave the message that the owner had good taste, the time to spend clipping or the money to pay someone else to do it, and could afford to grow box bushes as opposed to cabbages.

Dutch garden owners and makers have also had a long history of popularizing the formal French style; the construction of Het Loo coincided with French designer Daniël Marot publishing pattern books that were widely read by the newly wealthy merchants and landowners of Holland and the surrounding provinces, while a book of 1669 titled *Den Nederlandtsen Hovenier* (The Dutch Gardener) by the Royal Gardener Jan van der Groen provided 200 model plans for parterres, borders and other layouts. The royal family clearly saw no reason for keeping their style to themselves – another sign of the country's relative egalitarianism.

Fundamentally, though, there was perhaps another reason why the Baroque look took off in Holland and stayed at the heart of Dutch popular garden culture, more so than elsewhere; it has to do with the exceptional nature of the country and its culture, in particular the role that landscape management and horticulture have had.

In a landscape that was being increasingly planned and engineered, it was natural to plan and engineer the plants too: avenues, plantations, roadside trees, all were increasingly disciplined into straight lines with trees at regular intervals. The horticultural interests that all urban Europe began to develop with the growth of increasingly prosperous cities from the 17th century onwards were concentrated in Holland and its neighbouring provinces where wealthy urbanites, restrained from investing in country properties by the shortage of land, instead lavished their wealth on beautiful houses, art and gardening. Basic garden awareness and horticultural skills became widespread, and deeply culturally rooted.

01

03

02

04

The classical geometry of the garden style shown off so superbly at Het Loo has remained ever popular across a wide range of countries. It has largely lost its aristocratic associations, although it still speaks loudly and clearly of 'heritage'. Arguably, only once has it really been successfully reinvented, in the sense of taking the basic concept and moving it on – and that was in The Netherlands, and was largely the work of garden and landscape designer Mien Ruys, who took the techniques of clipping and the basic geometric forms and did something quite different with them, creating a style unmistakably different and clearly part of something larger, the Modernist movement in design.

05

06

01
Precision pruning.

02
The parterre with its coloured gravels.

03
A canal and gazebo.

04
The Fountain of Venus.

05
Planted urns as wall finials.

06
The outer, more informal, garden area at Het Loo.

07
The recreated green cabinet, made originally for the queen (Mary Stuart).

08
The recreated parterres of Het Loo, with some modern planting.

09
A view from above shows the clear and elegant lines of the parterres.

07

INSPIRED BY LANDSCAPE DESIGNERS

GARDENS UNDER BIG SKIES

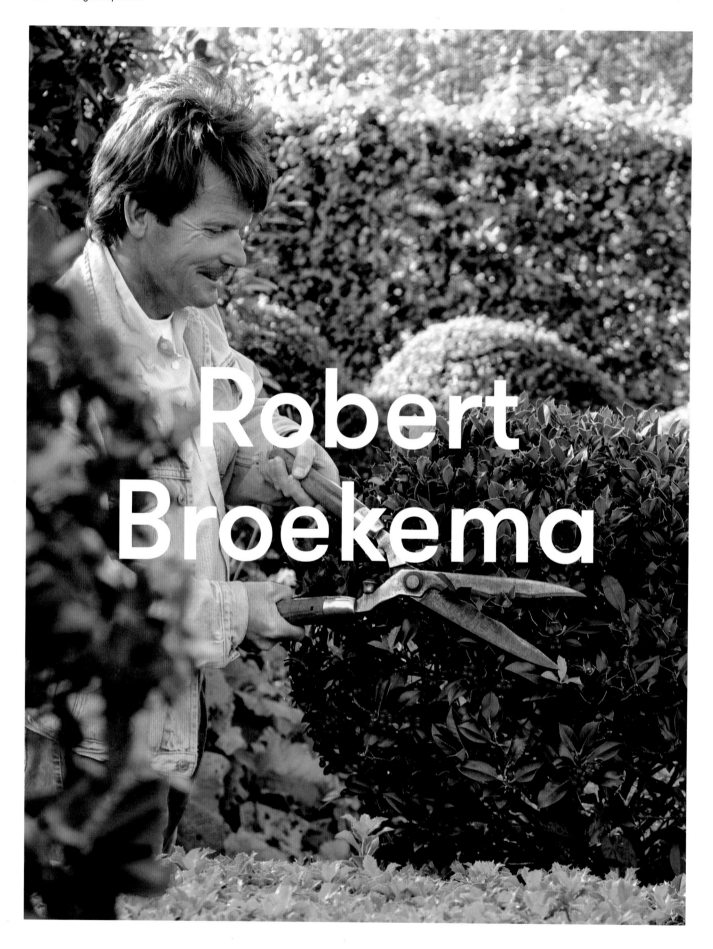

Robert
Broekema

Tourists flock past the elegant canal houses of Amsterdam's streets, largely without a thought as to what lies behind them. The gardens at the rear are a world apart: quiet, secluded, secret. Walled off from the often busy streets by the houses, together they can form quite large green blocks and include many mature trees. A pioneer in planning regulations, the city government passed a law in 1615 to protect these spaces from commercial development or further building. Known as *keurblokken*, there are 27 protected blocks within the historic canal neighbourhood, and in particular between the two called Keizersgracht and Herengracht; the gardens within them are known as *keurtuinen*.

Garden designer Robert Broekema works in a variety of different styles and in town and country, but there is a feeling that the *keurtuinen* are his natural habitat. Indeed, he has designed many gardens in the central area of the city. After studying Landscape and Architecture at Van Hall Larenstein University of Applied Sciences and working in a number of jobs and apprenticeships in Germany and the UK, including for Mien Ruys in Dedemswaart, he started out on his own, getting off to a very good start with designing a garden on the prestigious Herengracht in 1990 – one that was 18 m (59 ft) wide and 40 m (131 ft) long, as generous as they come in this densely populated area. Many more commissions in the area followed.

Robert's design work runs through the spectrum from classical to informal and naturalistic, but always with a clear framework and a definite tendency towards a style that if not minimalist is at least a disciplined approach that follows strongly the design motto of 'less is more'.

If we see the formality of Het Loo as a kind of gene in the Dutch garden subconscious, then Robert's work can be regarded as the expression of that gene at an ever-decreasing dilution and given an ever-widening creative interpretation. Classical formality is an obvious and traditional solution as to what to do in small town gardens, the lines and angles repeating those of the architecture, but Robert says, 'I prefer the more natural; formality in some spaces can be boring.' Indeed, there is a limit as to what can be done using only straight lines and right angles. A more modernist expression of these traditional lines eschews the hedges and clear focal points, and instead tends to work with blocks. In some of Robert's city gardens these blocks are used along axes and at regular intervals, interspersed with perennials, creating a strong rhythm. Another similar element in some of his gardens is lines of paving slabs set in grass with gaps between them; in an otherwise very informal country garden this is almost like the final and most diluted expression of the Het Loo design gene.

01

01
Low box cubes are the start of this Amsterdam garden's axis.

02
Hosta 'Francis Williams' and *Dryopteris filix-mas*.

03
A fern flourishes in a shaded container.

04
Clipped balls of yew, *Taxus baccata*.

02

04

03

01

INSPIRED BY LANDSCAPE DESIGNERS

An important element in understanding any formal garden, particularly one in a small space, is the concept of the *coulisse*, the word given to the painted panels of scenery that stand at the side of the stage in theatres. The Renaissance origins of the European formal garden lie with Italian theatre designers, and in the form of narrow screens of beech, coulisses appear in some of Robert's gardens; more informally, a tall shrub at the side can perform the same function. Coulisses tempt the eye, suggesting to the viewer that there is more to be seen or that something is to be expected. A bigger version of the coulisse does not just conceal but redirects the feet as well as the eye and can even direct the visitor to another compartment of the garden altogether; in one of Robert's gardens a very formal layout balances the architecture of an unusually wide house (for Amsterdam), but a narrow entrance to another part reveals an area of a very different character, on another axis.

The central axis, that all-important spine of the classical formal garden, can emphasize distance, but this is not always the case. In a short garden it may emphasize the limitations of the garden space instead, or in a very narrow one, contribute to a feeling of being hemmed in. There are circumstances, however, where the axis can be used to novel effect.

A real masterpiece is a design of Robert's where three different home-owners agreed to combine their gardens. All maintain a certain distinctive character of their own, but the three (each one about 6m or 20 ft across) meld into each other remarkably seamlessly: one is quite flowery, with perennials, the middle one is relatively simple, while the next is also quite simple but with a bit more planting.

The crucial linking factor is a central axis that cuts across the gardens at right angles in the form of a long, narrow pool. Paving slab paths turn into steps to cross it, so it never becomes a barrier; seen from one of the long ends of the pool, however, the slabs in the pool read more as subtle divisions of it than as routes across.

Gardens of the Baroque era displayed their flowering plants as individual specimens, choice objects to reflect glory on the taste, wealth and good connections of the owner. Plants do not have such status today, and those who have any familiarity

'When I started out I used a lot of English-style borders,' Robert says. 'English gardens were my main inspiration, but now I try to create gardens that have a longer season, with a more strategic use of evergreens and big groups of perennials or grasses that make an impact over an extended period.'

with plants and gardens are less easy to impress. One way round this is to plant multiples and make an impact, although this only works with those plants that have a long season and look good after flowering. 'When I started out I used a lot of English-style borders,' Robert says. 'English gardens were my main inspiration, but now I try to create gardens that have a longer season, with a more strategic use of evergreens and big groups of perennials or grasses that make an impact over an extended period.' This approach works well with hostas, which have good-quality foliage from late spring to autumn. The perennials can be a feature in their own right, while others are less emphatic, such as *Geranium macrorrhizum*, but offer a matt fresh green appearance that contrasts well with other plants. Yet others do not naturally lend themselves to this style of planting – *Salvia yangii* (formerly *Perovksia atriplicifolia*) has a rather wayward air with long, rangy stems that do not always go where we feel they should, but for midsummer, when the number of flowering perennials is relatively low, it works and arguably massing it like this is the most effective way of displaying it.

Blocks of grasses feature in the larger-scale and more contemporary gardens. They are grown not just for their flowerheads and seedheads, which is really the only function they have in so many naturalistic gardens, but also, or even primarily, for the impact they have as single-species blocks, where there is an interesting combination of the shape of the block with the softness of the grass foliage. Robert likes to use *Miscanthus sinensis* 'Gracillimus' – indeed Mien Ruys was one of the pioneers of this particular use of what is an elegantly tidy, generally non-flowering cultivar; he also incorporates forms of *Molinia caerulea*.

01
Two completely different gardens, both designed by Robert.

The crucial linking factor is a central axis that cuts across the gardens at right angles in the form of a long, narrow pool. Paving slab paths turn into steps to cross it, so it never becomes a barrier; seen from one of the long ends of the pool, however, the slabs in the pool read more as subtle divisions of it than as routes across.

01

01
Three merged gardens.

02
Widely spaced paving slabs emphasize the green of the lawn.

03
Lythrum salicaria 'Blush'.

04
The most richly planted of the three gardens.

02

04

03

05

06

07

08

05
Hydrangeas have become an essential part of Dutch gardens.

06
Festuca glauca and *Heuchera villosa* 'Palace Purple'.

07
The soft green of *Alchemilla mollis*.

08
The pool cuts across the axes of the three gardens.

01

Like all garden designers, Robert works to client briefs, and there is no doubt that many people want the predictability of classical formality. For those who don't, the notion that a long, narrow garden has to obey certain traditional rules is challenged by designers like Robert. Instead of a central axis, he may choose a pathway that wends between shrubs and perennials; each block of planting tends to have a clipped shrub, very often a box, as its backbone, most likely to be cut in a rounded shape. In fact, many clients now prefer softer shapes. Robert explains, 'If people have a stressful working life, they want something more relaxing, and over the last seven years I have begun to create softer gardens with more curves. Piet Oudolf has made a big impact and many clients want his more naturalistic look, while I want to move on from traditional formality where the straight lines of the architecture dictate all the lines and forms of the garden. I have a small garden plot near the Amstel in which there isn't a straight line. I find that more creative, more satisfying – you can do a lot with straight lines and they make design very easy, but I like having more of a challenge working with softer lines.'

Planting in the less formal gardens can become lush. The deeply urban setting of a town garden can seem almost like a challenge to create as much greenery as possible, one that Robert rises to with confidence. While much of his planting maintains an air of cool minimalism about it, he can also work with dense plantings, where different species grow closely together. The area of walls in narrow gardens may add to more than the surface area of the garden itself, so climbers offer many possibilities. Some of Robert's gardens make use of the self-clinging *Hydrangea petiolaris* and ivy (*Hedera* spp.) as a green coating for walls. In one particular small town garden, the paths are as narrow as possible, with a wide variety of planting, foliage dominating – as indeed it nearly always does in his designs. A Japanese maple, a bamboo, *Fatsia japonica* and even a *Gunnera manicata* are all here. Too daring to put all this into such a small garden? It works, perhaps because there is a rich understorey of less visually demanding plants that gives them context. Interestingly, here there is not a single trace of formality; the strong foliage forms make it

In fact, many clients now prefer softer shapes. Robert explains, 'If people have a stressful working life, they want something more relaxing, and over the last seven years I have begun to create softer gardens with more curves. Piet Oudolf has made a big impact and many clients want his more naturalistic look, while I want to move on from traditional formality where the straight lines of the architecture dictate all the lines and forms of the garden.'

01
The plan of one of Robert's gardens.

unnecessary, and indeed if you can imagine the garden without the plants, the paths would still give it a strong structure; formal planting here might even be over-egging the pudding.

    A life along the canals inevitably leads to a concern for the future of the area, to protect its heritage but also to encourage good use of space. Robert is involved with the Foundation for Amsterdam Canal Gardens, a small group dedicated to the celebration and conservation of the gardens of the area. They organize an annual three-day series of open days every third week of June.

Originally yards which were often used for drying and bleaching linen and clothes, with perhaps only a few herbs or choice flowers, the canal gardens of Amsterdam have developed a rich garden culture since the 17th century, and Robert's contribution to this culture has helped it to develop in diverse and creative new directions.

02

03

04

02
Curving paths and dense planting.

03
Gunnera manicata and *Rodgersia pinnata*.

04
A small town garden can be a botanical oasis.

05
A centrally placed *Acer palmatum* 'Atropurpureum' with *Hydrangea petiolaris* on the wall to the left.

06
Fatsia japonica is ideal for town gardens.

INSPIRED BY LANDSCAPE DESIGNERS

06

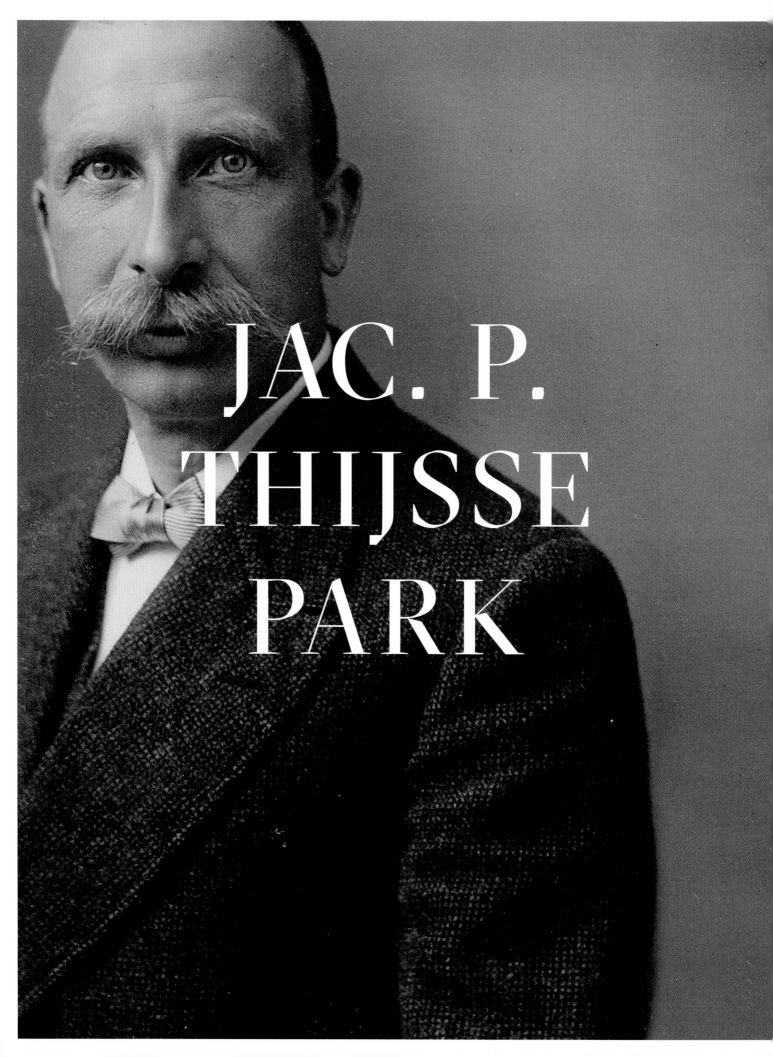

JAC. P. THIJSSE PARK

Sheets of pure white wood anemones *(Anemone nemorosa)* cover the ground, really about as far as the eye can see, before they disappear in a haze of twigs and fresh green emerging leaves. Further on, there are masses of pink corydalis *(Corydalis solida)*, and primroses *(Primula vulgaris)*. Later, there will be bluebells *(Hyacinthus non-scriptus)* which we are perhaps a little more used to seeing on this woodland floor-smothering scale. The spectacle is deeply impressive, especially once we realize that some of these plants, for example the anemones, take years to establish in our own gardens, and so this spread must represent a very considerable period of continual growth. We have to remind ourselves that this is a public park, not an ancient woodland.

In fact, it is a little too perfect to be a real ancient woodland; the consistency of the spring wild flower coverage is a little too exact, and there is an absence of the kind of scrubby bushes or patches of brambles that tend to break up the floor in most 'natural' woodland. These spring wild flowers are one of the special aspects of the parks in the town of Amstelveen, effectively a suburb of Amsterdam, and remarkably close to busy Schiphol Airport. Built in stages between 1939 and 1972, and following a series of waterways that wend their way through residential areas, the parks are wonderfully peaceful retreats from the city, with networks of paths that lead the visitor through woodland glades, along the shores of pools and among a complex patchwork of different habitats. Environments that probably appear completely natural to many of their visitors are in fact nothing of the sort, as all have been deliberately constructed from former agricultural land and are intensively managed.

The spring wild flowers disappear in due course, and the woodland floor becomes largely forgotten beneath the lush growth of the trees. In more open areas, however, there are other wild flowers, mostly woodland edge or meadow species such as red campion *(Silene dioica)*, cranesbill *(Geranium pratense)* and burnet *(Sanguisorba officinalis)*. They too are just a bit too perfect to be really wild – their density is higher than would be seen in 'nature' – and there is little of the grass that normally dominates the vegetation in open habitats, or of the brambles that often take over around woodland.

The diversity and the density of the flowering, colourful, attractive-to-the-human-eye vegetation gives the whole place a sense of the hyper-real, as if this were a kind of stylized countryside, a more perfect nature.

This feeling carries on into the summer as well, even though there are few flowers and much of the ground is covered in a low, richly textured vegetation: heathers, bilberries and ferns, with dramatic and almost tropically luxuriant clumps of royal fern *(Osmunda regalis)*. Come autumn, with the browns, yellows and oranges of oak, alder and willow foliage, the parks take on perhaps their wildest aspect.

The Thijsse Park (or, more properly, the Dr Jac. P. Thijsse Park) is the best-known of the Amstelveen parks. Jac. Thijsse (1865–1945) was an educationalist, writer and early environmental campaigner, who recognized, long before others, that The Netherlands was losing all its wild nature. As well as writing books about gardening (including one about house plants) he wrote about nature, and the need to conserve what remained. One of his innovations was the 'instructive garden', a kind of neighbourhood botanical garden, where native plants were grown not in a formal garden way but as part of reconstructed natural plant communities, largely for the educational benefit of the public. Several such gardens were established in the 1920s and '30s but the Amstelveen parks set a radical new direction, creating highly artistic evocations of flower-rich vegetation on a landscape scale. They established a pattern for the making of 'heemparks' which use native plants and highlight the natural heritage of the increasingly industrialized countryside.

01

02

03

04

01
Thijsse was primarily known as a writer about nature and a conservationist.

02
Drifts of *Corydalis solida* in spring.

03
Primroses (*Primula vulgaris*) en masse.

04
Wood anemones (*Anemone nemorosa*).

05
Bluebells (*Hyacinthoides non-scripta*).

05

Constructed during the 1930s on peaty agricultural land, Amstelveen was a model suburb adjacent to the Bospark, an area of natural-style woodland which had also been laid out under the guidance of Thijsse.

The smaller parks in Amstelveen were the responsibility of Chris P. Broerse (1902–95), who experimented with planting wildflower communities based on the study of 'plant sociology', a well-established branch of botany in Germany which studies how plants group themselves in the wild; what combinations of species occur together, in what proportions and why. Recreating natural plant communities proved difficult, however, until Broerse learnt to do it 'the natural way', which has dominated the management of the parks ever since.

The way Broese identified was to embrace succession, a key concept in plant ecology which describes how plant communities develop over time on a predictable trajectory until they reach a climax, beyond which further development is no longer possible – usually in the form of a mature forest of some kind. All gardening and landscape management involves managing succession in some way, including mowing lawns, weeding and pulling out tree seedlings, but in nature, the succession of different plant communities varies according to soil conditions and aspect. Managing succession is a key part of the Amstelveen approach, accounting for much of its visual interest and its sense of 'naturalness'.

The plants here are almost all natives, though some of the bulbs and spring flowers are not: summer snowflake (*Leucojum aestivum*), snowdrops (*Galanthus nivalis*), *Corydalis* and golden aconite (*Eranthis hyemalis*). Here, and indeed elsewhere in The Netherlands, they are treated as honorary natives and are known as *stinzenplanten*, or 'stone house plants'. They are mainly bulb, tuber and root crops that were planted from around the 16th century in country estates and around castles and country houses. Larger estates tended to be located in the northern provinces of Groningen and Friesland; here these plants spread and naturalized, seeding into areas of lawn and in shaded ground beneath trees, becoming a much-loved feature of spring. They are now well-established as garden elements, their ability to spread by themselves, given time, and their ability to decorate the ground between larger perennials and shrubs before they have started growth being widely appreciated.

06
Greater burnet
(*Sanguisorba officinalis*),
a wild flower of summer
meadows.

07
Young fronds of
the royal fern
(*Osmunda regalis*).

08
Kingcup (*Caltha
palustris*), the earliest
wetland flower.

09
Red campion
(*Silene dioica*).

06

07

08

09

Many of the users of Thijssepark and other Amstelveen parks, notably de Braak, probably think that everything there is natural, but anyone familiar with nature will see that they might be better described as 'nature enhanced'. The density of the wild flowers is one giveaway, and the distinct visual character of different areas of vegetation from each other is another.

'We try to keep everything the way it is,' explains Walter Busse, the manager here. The prolific growth of tree seedlings is a major problem, 'but weed growth starts earlier now . . . we face many problems because of climate change. Areas also need occasional restoration.' This refers to a process that is essentially about 'resetting the clock' in terms of succession; much of the existing vegetation is removed, leaving a few strategic larger plants and bare peaty soil into which seeds are scattered of the smaller herbaceous plants that in nature would dominate the early stages of succession.

The years following restoration involve the seeding and spread of those herbaceous plants which naturally grow on peat or on disturbed ground, which include *Arnica montana, Campanula rotundifolia* and *Lychnis flos-cuculi*. They are soon replaced by sedges (*Carex* species) and the first heathers. It is the latter, and bilberries (*Vaccinium myrtillus*) that then take over and dominate for many years, until eventually tree seedlings would take over if the restoration process were not started again.

The management of the Amstelveen parks may be relatively intensive and geared towards keeping them very much the same, but that 'same' is like a series of snapshots of natural plant communities as they develop over time. This is one of the things that makes these parks such special environments – that there is a recognition of the aspect of time here and therefore this artistic representation of nature is in many ways a realistic one.

01
Star of Bethlehem
(*Ornithogalum*
umbellatum)
naturalizes easily in
a sunny spot.

Ornithogalum umbellatum 362

02
Meadow saxifrage
(Saxifraga granulata)
does best in moist
meadows with
loamy soil.

Saxifraga granulata L. 1656.

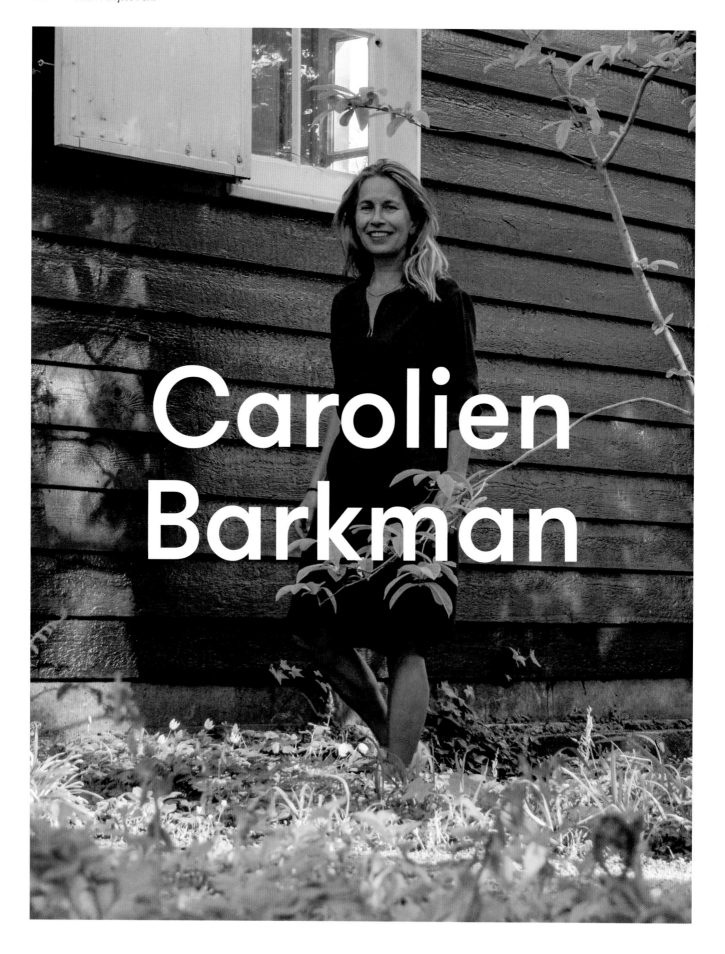

Carolien Barkman

'In high school I decided I wanted to be a garden designer, but my parents didn't think it was a very wise decision, as you couldn't earn much money doing that.' Substitute 'artist' or 'writer' for 'garden designer' and it is a familiar story, usually in the context of a successful creative person who has escaped a worthy but uninspiring professional life. Carolien Barkman did as she was advised, studying law and entering the legal profession, but 'always designing gardens on the side' – all the more impressive as she had three small children too. For her it was natural, probably almost instinctive: 'I was always interested in gardens. My mother is a keen gardener and I had a great grandfather who ran a nursery and an aunt who designed gardens,' she says. Carolien is known for her ability to perform miracles in tight spaces, nearly all city gardens. 'I have a reputation for small gardens,' she says. 'I never decided to concentrate on them, but that is what people always ask, although I would like to do a larger project one day.'

Generally, the more successful a garden designer becomes, the wealthier their clients are and so the bigger the gardens they are asked to design, but this is not the case in The Netherlands; from the Golden Age onwards, the relationship between wealth and area of land owned did not follow the same economic laws as in other countries. There was not much land to go round, so the rich invested in other areas instead, such as paintings. The result is that the design of small gardens is certainly at a higher level of expertise and creativity here than elsewhere.

'I went to school in Amstelveen,' says Carolien, 'and for drawing lessons we went to the parks, so I discovered them at a young age. I think they are magical, very subtle, and there's always something to enjoy at every season. I still love to go to them as I like the feeling of airiness, and there are very different areas, offering contrasting experiences.'

She particularly appreciates the filtered light through the trees, the transitions from sun to shade, and the way the plant species are sometimes together in groups but elsewhere are mixed. For someone who works overwhelmingly with perennials, this variation in planting strategies must be of continual interest. However, she also has her criticisms, feeling they are a little too manicured, and agrees with a description of them as 'hypernature'. For a working designer, though, this 'cultivated nature' may be of more value as inspiration than unrestricted nature, which is usually so unlike anywhere cultivated that few are able to gain useful lessons in planting design from it.

'In small gardens, every detail, every plant counts,' Carolien says. 'In city gardens there is always a shady part and a sunny part, so planting has to reflect that, and I see it as a challenge to make it as green as possible.'

01
A corner of a small square garden.

02
Planting in a shaded space, inspired by woodland-floor habitat.

An important aspect of the Amstelveen parks for Carolien is what happens beneath your feet. 'There are different surfaces to walk on – tarmac, gravel, woodchip – and they have an impact on how you experience your surroundings,' she says. Such differences are crucial to making the most of small gardens, where every sensory detail is valuable. She also says that she likes 'the slightly messy parts, like when *Verbascum* starts to grow by itself.' This love of spontaneity is something that she tries to translate into her gardens by sowing some annuals and other short-lived species between those that she puts in as plants.

When Carolien made her decision in the mid 1990s to give up the law and become a garden designer, she spent a year following a course by the landscape architect Frits van Loon, followed by a year in a nursery and then a year with a company that undertakes the physical work of installing gardens. She says, 'Since then, I have often seen courses I would like to do, to get a proper education, but I am too busy

working.' Perhaps it is part of Carolien's strength that she has not learnt the clichés or got stuck in the ruts of established ways of doing things. Indeed, her secret is to go slightly off course. 'I grew up in an old polder district,' she recalls. 'The ditches seem to be straight lines, but actually never are. I like the disorder in them, the fact that there are plants growing in the ditches that put themselves there. Some of them even block the view, so not everything is obvious at first.' She describes the pattern made by the repetition of the ditches as creating a rhythm, but for her 'there is always something just disturbing it. I like that. I put it into my design work, but I only see it when I have finished, and I say to myself "I did it again." So many designers work in a very regular way, everything very straight, everything in order, they take lines out from the house, and use them as a basis for design.'

While she adds that there's nothing wrong with that, clearly she prefers not to design in that way. As an example she talks about 'pathways that widen, then narrow, then go a little bit to the left, although at first sight they look straight'. She goes on to describe how she quite often does little things that don't quite match up, or repeats

features that don't fit together as we would expect them to. Some might see these as mistakes, and perhaps the fact that Carolien regards them as an integral part of what she does shows a deep inner confidence. In fact there is a parallel: in Japan, widely seen as the world's leading design culture, much of its best design falls slightly short of perfect regularity. Like Carolien's work, it makes a virtue out of asymmetry.

'In small gardens, every detail, every plant counts,' Carolien says. 'In city gardens there is always a shady part and a sunny part, so planting has to reflect that, and I see it as a challenge to make it as green as possible.'

One way of maximizing green is with vertical planting, using climbers. Indeed the value of climbers in city gardens is greatly underestimated, and their use is perhaps limited by the fears some have of them damaging buildings – fears that research in Germany has indicated are greatly exaggerated. Given the spectacular colours some climbers have in the autumn, they can also be a very good way of celebrating the seasons. Gardens designed by Carolien

03
Containers,
including one simply
with duckweed.

04
A curving path makes
the most of the space
between the house and
a boundary.

05
A long, narrow
garden broken up
with planting.

include one where perennials foam around an off-centre square of paving, bordered by decking; in another, perennials, shrubs and climbers explore and exploit every available space around the walls of a central Amsterdam garden, which before her intervention must have felt profoundly overwhelmed by the surrounding buildings. The tiny paved garden of the house where she used to live had an array of pots with plants of varying sizes, and even two bowls of water with the surface completely covered in duckweed.

Planting is hugely important for Carolien. The current fashion for perennials is perfect for her, as small gardens have to rely on them for most of their interest. 'I experiment in every garden,' she says. 'There are always so many new plants to try – I take the advice of the nursery where I've always bought my plants.'

A favourite, with the loose but distinctive shape that encapsulates the qualities she particularly likes in perennials, is *Astilboides tabularis*, which has expansive heads of cream flowers with a slightly wayward quality, as well as unusual and

stylish circular leaves. 'But,' she says, 'if you have clients who are not good at maintenance you provide anemones, persicarias, geraniums – plants that are totally predictable.' Her love of sowing in some self-seeding species is something that few other designers do, possibly fearing unpredictable consequences. It provides a 'light natural touch' and that element of dissonance that she values so highly.

In discussing influences, Carolien says she likes 'the designs of Gilles Clément – they look natural and he is very good at making designs with plants that are very specific for that place – and of course Dan Pearson and Sarah Price. And I grew up with Mien Ruys; I like her frameworks but the planting is too bold for me.' She makes a comparison with Piet Oudolf, 'who I also grew up with – he makes planting more subtle, more magical'. She describes how she likes graphic qualities in gardens, referencing the De Stijl movement and designers such as Gerrit Rietveld – but the artist she admires most is Jan Schoonhoven (1914–44), known for his abstract cardboard reliefs (usually with a subtle imperfection). This appreciation of the graphic is important as a balance to her love of plants, especially of naturalistic perennials.

Designing is a highly intuitive business. Carolien says, 'When I first meet clients, I like it when they have references. I look at the house, at the interior, I look at them . . . it usually takes me an hour and then I have an idea about what to do. The design, though, is not something I can do in an hour – it takes a long time, like a puzzle. It has to grow, and takes about a month on average. I think about it, I come back to it, I think about it again, I come back to it . . . I draw a little, but really I design in my head, as sometimes things come to me suddenly.'

The variation in size and aspect of urban gardens and the wide range of suitable plants means that Carolien has many variables to play with, so her gardens not surprisingly tend to be very different from each other. In all of them, though, there will be that little twist of the unexpected, the dissonant note that reminds us that perfection can be dull.

01

02

03

04

01
A square garden given
interest through
distorting the square.

02
Geranium 'Ivan'.

03
The meadow effect
for a small space.

04
Allium nigrum, a
robust tall garlic.

05
The diagonal view in
a small garden is
always important.

05

01

02

03

04

05

01
Orthogonal geometry
with a range of
textures and colours.

02
Aruncus 'Horatio'.

03
Hesperis matronalis.

04
The plan of a garden
in Amsterdam.

05
Soleirolia soleirolii with
decking and paving.

06
A variety of surfaces
enriches the experience
of stepping.

07
Digitalis lutea, an upright
plant for light shade.

08
Fingerleaf or rodgers
flower (*Rodgersia*).

09
Geranium macrorrhizum,
a stalwart for shade.

06

07

08

09

01

03

01
Containers can be
used to make multiple
micro-habitats.

02
A close-up of *Sparmannia
africana*, a house
plant standing out for
the summer.

03
*Thalictrum
aquilegifolium.*

04
Wildflower and common
'weed' *Geranium
robertianum* even
does well in shade.

05
Views from above
are important in
town gardens.

02

04

05

01

01
A corten steel pond with spring perennials and *Tulipa* 'Spring Green'.

02
Anemone blanda 'Blue Shades'.

03
Dryopteris erythrosora.

04
Saxifraga × urbium.

05
Viburnum opulus 'Roseum'.

06
Hyacinthoides non-scripta.

07
Euphorbia amygdaloides var. robbiae.

08
Geranium macrorrhizum.

09
Brunnera macrophylla.

01

02

01
Hyacinthoides hispanica,
the paler Spanish bluebell.

02
Climbers and small
beds distract the eye
along the axis of a long
narrow space.

03
Leucojum aestivum and
a water container.

04
Tiarella cordifolia
'Oakleaf', a shade-lover.

05
Omphalodes cappadocica
'Starry Eyes', a
groundcover plant for
shade.

06
Pruned beech keeps its
leaves in winter.

07
Spiraea × arguta, a
very free-flowering
shrub for spring.

03

04

05

06

07

MIEN RUYS
AND THE
CONTEMPORARY
GARDEN

Walking around the Tuinen Mien Ruys near the town of Dedemsvaart in the eastern Netherlands, there is an odd familiarity. The perennials, and the strong lines of much of the design, remind one of early Piet Oudolf projects, and there is a distinct feeling of 'so this is where he came from'. There is also a definite reminder of other designers who established their reputation in the latter part of the 20th century, John Brookes in the UK for one: so much follows a grid, often dictated by square paving slabs, with a confident and unapologetic use of modern materials (concrete, railway sleepers) and a sense that although plants are enjoyed, understood and well used, they are subordinate to the overall, very simple, design.

Mien Ruys (1904–99) dominated Dutch garden and landscape design in the second half of the 20th century. While she was undoubtedly a genius, she was also the right person in the right place at the right time. She started her career in the 1920s, when landscape design was undeveloped; she came into her own after World War II, when reconstruction, followed by the growing economic success of the country during the 1950s, created enormous opportunities for the young garden design industry, with a zeitgeist that was open to innovation and creative thinking. She was not just a very good designer but was also in a strong position to play an important role in creating and moulding the new industry.

The overall impression of Tuinen Mien Ruys is of simple, bold, graphic lines, spaces and volumes – clearly a part of the post-Bauhaus modern movement.

Seeing examples of earlier work by landscape architects, and garden designers even more so, can be problematic as so much of it gets altered over time, often affected negatively, or overlaid by the work of others. In the case of Mien Ruys, however, we have a remarkable example that records her thinking, planning and construction methods over her entire career. The grounds of her lifelong home, where she tried out and refined many of her smaller-scale ideas, Tuinen Mien Ruys gives a unique window into her imagination, especially when she worked on design concepts for the smaller post-war garden. It is remarkable how few garden and landscape designers have a place of their own to experiment on any meaningful scale, or indeed the desire to do so. Piet Oudolf's garden at Hummelo and Roberto Burle Marx's property outside Rio de Janeiro come to mind; that they have towering reputations too is perhaps an indication that to have one's own trial plot is a great benefit that many miss out on.

The overall impression of Tuinen Mien Ruys is of simple, bold, graphic lines, spaces and volumes – clearly a part of the post-Bauhaus modern movement.

There is no trace of any traditional garden features, yet there is plenty of formality in the clipped shrubs, most of them the conventional yew and box, but some novel and experimental, such as a form of purple-leaved *Berberis thunbergii*. These are all arranged in unfamiliar ways: yew blocks that stand next to each other but get progressively narrower, or three low box blocks scattered randomly across a paved terrace, their dimensions a neat multiple of that of the paving. Then there are grasses which are treated in formal ways too, as if they were hedging or freestanding blocks.

There are however a lot of perennials, including some quite conventional borders, but as they have their place and have stayed in it, the overall impression is of a plan and everything having its appointed location. Mien Ruys's father had been one of the country's leading commercial growers of perennials, and she herself wrote several books about using perennials in gardens. The ones she favoured, though, were those with a definite graphic quality about them, *Phlomis russeliana*, with its broad ground-hugging leaves and sturdy flower/seedheads, being a good example.

01

02

01
Mien Ruys was an early
user of grasses.

02
The use of decay-resistant
plastics to construct
boardwalks was one of her
many innovations.

01
Patterns are frequently
dictated by grids.

02
Low-maintenance
areas with gravel.

03
A calm circle made
with wood sorrel
(Oxalis acetosella).

04
Boardwalks encourage
exploration.

02

01

03

04

Not surprisingly, Piet Oudolf was hugely influenced by Mien Ruys. Indeed, when he talks about his career he will say that when he started out 'there was only Mien Ruys', by which he means that she so completely dominated the world of garden and landscape design that it was very difficult to think of any other way of doing things.

John Brookes never visited Mien Ruys, but the similarity of his work suggests to us an important point – that both he and Mien Ruys were modernists, and so shared a perspective that was very different to garden design in the English-speaking world, which never really had a modernist phase and has found it difficult to stop endlessly returning to old Romantic models. This goes some way towards explaining why, despite similarities of climate and garden flora, the modern Dutch garden

nearly always looks very different to British and American ones.

Ruys studied widely in her youth, working for a nursery and garden construction company in England (during which time she met Gertrude Jekyll, generally regarded as one of the most influential planting designers of all time), as well as working in Germany. At the Delft Technical Institute, she met young architecture students who interested her in the social aspects of housing and the

05
Phlomis russeliana,
a quintessential
Mien Ruys plant.

06
Yew clipped in a
modernist style.

07
Early spring crocuses,
in regular formation.

08
Wide circles are
one of the typical
Mien Ruys shapes.

05

06

07

08

importance of urbanism – thinking about the townscape as a whole, subordinating architecture and landscape to an overall concept. This appealed to her radical politics and sense of justice, so although she continued to work for wealthy private clients, most of her energy went into public and communal spaces.

She started to work on urban projects in the early 1930s, creating communal gardens that used perennials in a way that would be regarded as too labour-intensive today. During the Nazi Occupation she began to teach, and in 1950, she and her husband Theo Moussault founded *Onze Eigen Tuin* (*Our Own Garden*), a magazine which still exists today. During the 1950s she not only worked on public projects but also established close relationships with a number of architects, as Jekyll had done with Edwin Lutyens. Her public gardens included some designed for factories, schools and hospitals; for her, it was a sign of being a civilized and caring society that everyone had a right to live and work in a high-quality designed environment. Her collaborations with architects and designers led to an informal circle of people who were all concerned with modern design and the social aspects of their work. Such élite circles have rarely involved garden or landscape designers, although the Bornim Circle of Karl Foerster in Weimar Germany also comes to mind.

Grids appear frequently in Ruys's work, and the sense of garden and landscape design being somehow subordinate to the lines and angles of buildings is somehow always there, as if Piet Mondrian's grid-based paintings had somehow influenced the brains of all designers of the pre-war period. However, she was famous for her oblique lines and her use of diagonals to divide space; she even acquired the nickname 'diagonal Mien'. In a culture where we tend to think in terms of axes and right angles, these obliques can sometimes be disconcerting, but they also add a quirky jolt to the way the viewer looks at a garden or other space. Such deviations from the norm disrupt viewers' expectations and make them look more carefully.

The innovative use of modern materials by Mien Ruys was another key aspect of her work but one which today is difficult to appreciate, as we have become so used to these materials and in some cases see them as clichés, even as old-fashioned or, as in the case of creosote-soaked railway sleepers, a health hazard. She experimented with using concrete in gardens to replace expensive and inevitably imported stone, developing some attractive materials involving gravel aggregate as a result. It was she who also popularized the use of railway sleepers as structural or even seating elements in gardens. All of this helped in the process of democratizing the post-war garden, since much pre-war middle-class gardening had involved the employment of staff, which was now far less likely to be the case; gardens not only shrank but had to be of low and simple maintenance. She even worked on modular borders so that clients could have well-designed borders without having to work out the planting themselves or pay a gardener to do it for them.

Mien Ruys was very prolific at all aspects of her work, and not surprisingly shaped the thinking of a generation of designers. The fact that some of her ideas have become a cliché is almost a back-handed compliment to her success. Above all, her stress on simple, clean lines, the maximizing of a sense of space and her adventurous plant usage helped a generation to create a democratic garden culture where anyone with a small outdoor space could do something to enhance it and make the most of it.

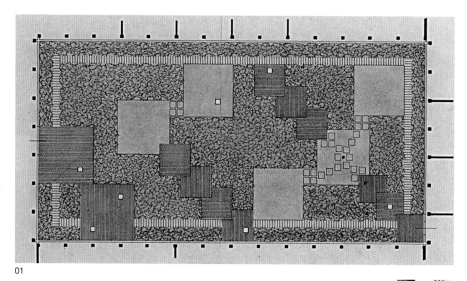

01

02

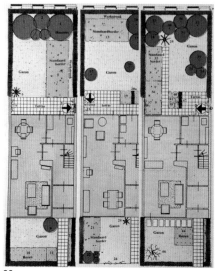

03

04

05

06

07

08

09

10

11

01
A plan for a factory garden, 1950s.

02
Mien Ruys designed many residential areas in the post-war era.

03
Plans of gardens for a row of houses.

04
Well-designed open space as a democratic right.

05
Box integrated with paving.

06
Miscanthus grass and a pool.

07
Precise matching of geometry is a typical touch.

08
Berberis thunbergii, one of many experimental hedge materials.

09
Traditional yew hedge given a modern twist.

10
Railway sleepers, one of Mien Ruys's most widely copied innovations.

11
Industrial cement piping used to make a pond.

Nico Kloppenborg

Once one has some familiarity with Mien Ruys's work, one sees her everywhere; she has clearly made an enormous impact on the entire garden culture of the contemporary Netherlands. Nico Kloppenborg, a garden designer who is based in Friesland in the north-west of the country, is clear about his own debt to her, and states it boldly. 'I have been very influenced by Mien Ruys, especially earlier in my career,' he says. 'She uses such bright lines, and she is very simple, very functional.' He goes on to discuss how much he has learnt from her, stressing certain lessons, each one of them a simple statement. What feels like lesson number one is that 'a fundamental is to search for the longest line in your garden – especially in a small garden'.

Many designers probably do this almost instinctively, as it marks the greatest extension of the garden. Making it clear and working from it as at least a conceptual axis will have the effect of maximizing perception of the space. Nico recommends using it as a basis for planning other garden features and running other axes and sight lines off it. This line is often oblique, the diagonal being the furthest extension of the rectangle – the garden designer's version of the bishop's move in a chess game.

'Mien Ruys always used to plant a tree in every garden she did, even if it was really small,' Nico recalls. He implies that sometimes people think she might have planted too many, and his own use of trees is judicious. Certain garden features invented or used frequently by Ruys that appear in his work, however, are concrete upside-down U-shaped blocks to sit on, wooden seating platforms just above the water level of a pool, and sunken seating areas; 'You are out of the wind and have more privacy,' he explains. He also uses bold planting, as Ruys did: 'She liked big leaves, *Petasites,* bold effects, the planting of big groups of one kind, the simplicity of something like one *Persicaria,* one willow tree and one ornamental grass.'

Nico has restored several Mien Ruys gardens over the years, but feels he often has to simplify them for contemporary clients, although he says 'I always keep her lines. Basic structure is so important, you must be able to, and want to, walk easily through a garden. Another thing I learnt from Mien is to structure the garden with hedging, and to make clear boundaries.'

As a child, Nico had his own little garden in that of his grandparents, his grandfather being a key inspiration as a grower of dahlias and sweet peas, as well as being a beekeeper. 'I still feel as if I am a child playing with gardens,' he says.

He was brought up in the village of Baarn, east of Amsterdam, a community with a long tradition of aristocratic and villa gardens and a royal palace, Soestdijk, which has an extensive parkland landscape. He has a strong recollection of his first trip to Tuinen Mien Ruys at the age of 24. At the time he was working as a teacher, but four years later he decided to do what he had always enjoyed and became a garden designer. He did a course in garden history at Utrecht University, but recalls, 'I had a feeling that I knew so much already, although it helped me with ordering knowledge and with the physical aspects of restoration.'

From 1985 until 2005 Nico ran a design business with an older colleague, Lia Duinker. 'She was very Scandinavian-orientated, so 90 per cent of the garden had to be green,' he says. 'She was not trend-driven, she was very individualistic . . . we had a lot of chemistry and we did a lot of big gardens together.' They started their marketing by mailing all the dentists in the area, got five commissions, 'and it started from there'. They worked in a number of styles, including a version of ecological restoration. 'We would spread out clippings from the heath on the sandy soils in Drenthe,' he recalls, 'and then let the resulting seedlings of heather and grasses grow. From there we could manage that as a naturalistic garden that was also very low maintenance.'

As well as designing gardens, Nico has been involved in a variety of restoration projects. Friesland is very different to the more densely populated provinces to its south as there is more space, and historically there has been a history of wealthy landowners with estates, often with extensive areas of woodland. Many of these are now public spaces and Nico has worked on restoring four. These were all designed by a noted local landscape designer, Lucas Pieters Roodbaard (1782–1851), who worked very much in the informal English landscape style. Original layouts have long since been lost beneath the growth of young trees, water courses have silted up and structures such as

01

bridges have become dilapidated. Nico's role has been to advise on appropriate tree felling, new tree and shrub planting, the restoration of water bodies, and the shaping of the landscape to be a welcoming and functional public space.

Roodbaard was followed by another eminent local landscape designer, Gerrit Vlaskamp (1834–1906), who designed several villa gardens in Nico's home village of Mantgum. Nico has been involved in some local restoration work here too, but also in the design of some new gardens, which typically involve simple clipped foliage shapes and hedges. He has also developed a form of hedging using lime (*Tilia cordata*), which makes use of the fact that the trees' twigs are able to graft themselves together when tied; instead of being pruned, new branches are tied back into the base of the plant, where they bond, so a dense interwoven basket of stems is formed, quite unlike that of any other hedging tree. The result is remarkably strong, which Nico illustrates by throwing himself at the hedge and bouncing back out from it.

Since about 2000, Nico has been involved in designing gardens at Sint Anthony Gasthuis in the nearby city of Leeuwarden. A *gasthuis* is essentially the equivalent of the English almshouse, but this extensive site, with some 60 living units, now functions as an independent

retirement community. Over the years, much rebuilding and repurposing has been done, with a continual stream of small garden projects. It is a complex site, and any garden-making has to be very site-specific and adapt well to site conditions, existing trees, the needs of residents and so forth. Nico's other work often involves larger projects for private individual gardens, where the clear sight lines and bold interventions typical of Mien Ruys can be employed with no restriction. He likes to talk to architects before their plans are fixed, in particular 'the position of the windows – I like having them lower so that you can bring the garden into the house better'.

Nico is interesting to talk to about the current vogue for perennials. 'Another thing I learnt from Mien Ruys is don't do too much and remember that the garden's architecture is more important than your planting,' he says – in other words, basic structures, clean lines, and clear frameworks will all outlive planting.

The Mien Ruys technique of using big groups of plants with good long-season foliage still finds favour with him, although it is distinctly out of fashion with most other garden designers, who have perhaps seen too many clichéd and minimalist blocks of ground cover. Ruys tended to favour bold-leaved plants such as hostas and *Phlomis russeliana* and Nico also likes to use this technique, though with lower-growing grasses or *Carex* species that were not available in her day but are very much part of the contemporary garden scene. 'I don't want to be like the Victorians and gather plants from all over the world,' he says, adding that in his opinion there is a parallel between modern perennial gardens and 19th-century bedding plants. Everything grows quickly, he points out, which is ideal for impatient clients who want near-instant results but carries the danger that there are no woody plants for the future.

01
Beech hedging.

02
The large leaves of
Gunnera manicata.

GARDENS UNDER BIG SKIES

01

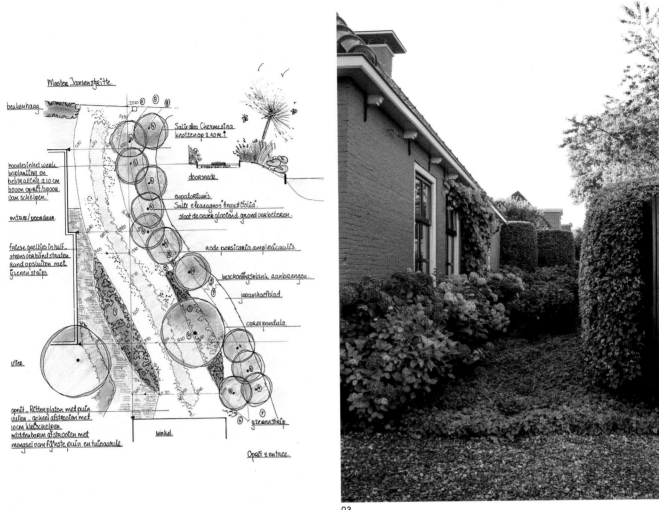

01
Barrels of hornbeam used as an alternative to a hedge.

02
Plan of the driveway.

03
For many people, summer is only summer if hydrangeas are present.

04
Nico likes imposing plants, here *Aralia californica* and *Thalictrum* 'Elin'.

01

02

Mien Ruys, who did much of her most important work during the 1950s when resources were limited, was very keen on using existing materials, a practice Nico follows, reusing bricks and tiles wherever possible. He also reuses plants – on one occasion at the Leeuwarden Gasthuis he dug up some existing hostas, divided them, spread them out over the ground and went over them with a rotovator to chop them up into small pieces, then sowed *Verbena bonariensis*. 'By August all was hosta and verbena. You should do gardening just like you do cooking. Ask yourself "what have I got in my refrigerator?" and use that. Don't go plant hunting in the nurseries,' he says.

Clipped hornbeam hedges play a major role in his own garden, which is unusual for a Dutch garden in being sited on a rise in the ground – in fact a terp which is the historic core of the village, with the church on its highest point. The visitor can recognize the house by its precisely clipped columns of hornbeam at the front, surrounded by perennial planting. At the back, simple foliage shapes predominate before making the descent down a series of hairpin bends defined by walls of clipped hornbeam, just high enough to almost obscure the view, but

not quite. 'We made the garden in one go, in 1998,' recalls Nico. 'Having bought some land below the property, we hired a crane and brought in some clay soil to build up the slope. We didn't plan it, there was no drawing – we just did it, directing the crane to where we wanted the soil.' The lowest part of the garden is dominated by what Nico describes as a 'bouquet' of birch trees, the result of a dozen planted in one hole. The ground is surfaced in slate and a number of robust perennials fill in around the outer rim. It is a secluded, quiet space, not at all intensively managed.

Some might find Nico's critique of an over-reliance on perennials old-fashioned, but his emphasis on the longevity of gardens that rely more on woody plants and inevitably take time to develop is refreshing, and somehow reassuring.

It may well be that future generations will be in a better position to judge. His emphasis on the principles of Mien Ruys's modernism are less controversial, and his clear summary of key points are ones that all designers can learn from.

01
Verbena bonariensis, an annual that usually self-seeds.

02
Verbena bonariensis is one of the best flowers for butterflies. Here a red admiral (*Vanessa atalanta*) has landed.

03
Clumps of *Miscanthus sinensis* 'Gracillimus' with *Phacelia tanacetifolia*.

GARDENS UNDER BIG SKIES

01
The sloping beech in
Nico's own garden.

02
The 'destination' of the
sloping path – the
bottom of the garden.

03
Carpinus columns
resembling menhirs make
a powerful year-round
statement.

04
Along the sloping path,
looking towards a *Catalpa
bignonioides* tree.

01

02

03

04

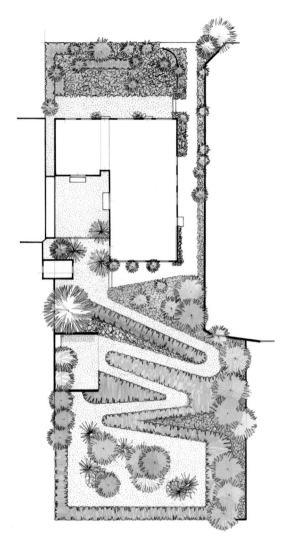

05

06

07

05
The plan of Nico's garden.

06
Looking back up
towards the house.

07
Another detail of the path
with surrounding beech.

01

01
There are few greens
fresher than those of
beech in spring.

02
Hornbeam, and, lower,
Lonicera ligustrina var.
yunnanensis 'Maigrün'.

03
The hornbeam columns –
clipping is a major
annual operation.

04
Slate fragments used as
a ground surface.

05
Hornbeam columns
against the house,
like buttresses.

02

03

04

05

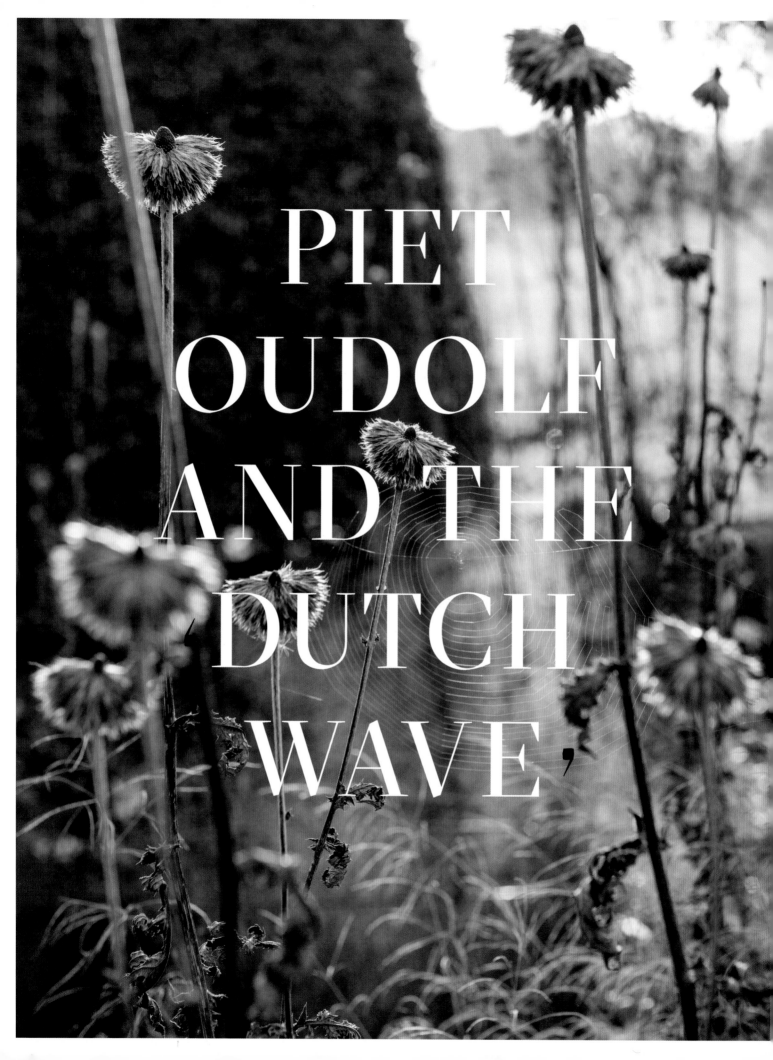

PIET OUDOLF AND THE 'DUTCH WAVE'

The crowds shuffle along the elevated walkway, coming to a halt if someone stops for too long – the usual reason being to take a photograph. It is the plants that flourish along the sides that attract people's attention, or sometimes the views out over the city from the height of around two storeys, or indeed the often artistically jarring juxtaposition of the two. Welcome to the New York High Line, which, since the first stage opened in 2009, has become one of the most popular visitor attractions in this city that has so many. The High Line has brought Piet Oudolf superstar status, and taken the latest in Dutch planting design to a global audience.

It is of course only the most unusual manifestation of an impressive body of work which has brought planting design to the attention of many who were largely unaware of it before, such as architects and the contemporary art community. Piet has also raised the profile of planting design with the landscape architecture profession, many members of which previously had shown little interest in this aspect of their work.

Piet's entire career has been in garden design, but the type of work he now carries out is almost entirely focused on planting. The spatial aspects of the projects he works on are developed by landscape designers and other professional groups, while the implementation he now mostly leaves to a select group of trusted colleagues such as Tom de Witte, all of whom have the passion about planting that he does. His planting style is the result, naturally, of continuous development over a long and successful career, but it is also directed, and arguably constrained, by the nature of his commissions and by client expectations.

Conversations with Piet during the 1990s inevitably reflected a sense of struggling to emerge from beneath the very strong influence of Mien Ruys; there was almost a feeling that she so dominated the field that it was difficult to think of new ways of putting plants together. His own garden at Hummelo in Gelderland originally incorporated the off-centre symmetry and the blocky clipped woody plants that spoke so loudly of her style. It was not just the occasional flood and the resulting fungal infections that saw these off; Piet himself had got bored with them and moved on to a more ambitious scale of perennial planting which gradually offered less of a role for them.

01

02

One reason for Piet's global profile is that he has been the most artistically successful member of a whole movement, variously called 'naturalistic planting', 'the new perennial movement' or even 'the Dutch wave'.

This movement brought together practitioners of garden and landscape design who wanted to prioritize ecological concerns (sustainability, bio-diversity, the use of native plants) with a revival of interest in herbaceous perennials, which had been immensely popular before World War II but had suffered a slow and continuous decline afterwards. Piet has often been described as 'the leading ecological designer', which is not the case at all as his driving motive is an artistic one, albeit firmly rooted in taking inspiration from natural plant communities. He does not have the passion for native plants, site-specific plant selection and wildlife that is shared by most of the practitioners in this movement, yet his work is far better regarding these concerns than most 'conventional' planting design: the plant selection is overwhelmingly of long-lived species, using small plants (both highly sustainable practices, in both the ecological and financial senses); there is huge diversity (good for nature) and the planting is sufficiently resilient that if maintenance is reduced, the plant combination will very often survive with remarkable tenacity. Hummelo itself is a good example of this, some plantings having remained largely untouched for nearly 30 years.

In his designs, Piet acts as an artist, with a highly intuitive approach to endless new formulations of an extensive plant palette. Crucial to understanding his work is to realize that it is primarily about plant structure rather than colour; a black and white photograph highlights this, as well as a considerable range of tone. At a superficial level, much of his planting design is relatively conventional in that it uses groups of plants of the same variety; however, their organization and structuring in space has a quality that is somehow electric and impossible to emulate. A crude statistical analysis points to a high proportion of species with a long season of good structure, and a lesser but very significant role for ornamental grasses.

01
Knautia seedlings, *Stipa gigantea*, *Salvia nemorosa* 'Caradonna', *Digitalis ferruginea*, *Euphorbia griffithii* 'Dixter', *Kniphofia* 'Alcazar', *Geranium* 'Rozanne', *Limonium latifolium*, *Nepeta* 'Souvenir d'André Chaudron'.

02
The perennial meadow, on the site of the former nursery.

03
Eupatorium maculatum in seed in late autumn.

04
Symphyotrichum 'Little Carlow' flowers well into the autumn.

05
Disintegrating seedheads of an *Echinops* species.

06
Seed heads of *Agastache nepetoides* and *Aster umbellatus*.

Following pages:
A view over the area for the mother plants in the former nursery.

01

The plant palette is relatively predictable, in that the same species tend to appear in most of his plantings; it may be seen as inflexible, but it is extremely reliable, and every project usually has some newer element, so it does slowly evolve. Piet's experience with growing the plants he uses gives his selections a quality that is lacking in the work of many other designers. For many years he and his wife, Anja, ran a small nursery, originally just to grow plants for the design business; growing plants commercially can also be a very good way of learning about their long-term performance. The nursery was established in the mid- to late 1980s, after the pair moved from their home area of Haarlem to the rural surroundings of Hummelo in Gelderland. His plant palette was largely crystallized during this time, a process which in many ways was a collaborative one, as his experiences with plants were shared extensively with other gardeners – most notably the late Henk Gerritsen, whom he credits with introducing him to the garden values of seedheads and the rewarding appearance of the plants post-flowering.

A second major influx of species to the Oudolf plant palette took place in the late 1990s, when he gained his first commissions in the US (the Lurie Garden, Chicago, and The Battery, New York) and began to explore prairie habitats in the Midwest, which made a huge impact on him. Public and professional interest in using American native species began to grow during the time, becoming a virtual tidal wave by the 2010s; local practitioners came under heavy pressure to use only natives. Piet, however, was in a strong position to show how natives and introduced species could be highly successful together.

02

03

Herbaceous perennials overwhelmingly dominate Oudolf plantings, especially since his projects have tended to become bigger, either because they are for wealthy clients with a lot of space or are public spaces; there is little doubt that the latter are his preference. The 'big expanse of perennial' is a style that fits into big-sky landscapes or urban settings, such as the plantings he has done on the old waterfront area in Rotterdam. Given surrounding shrub planting, it can be more intimately contextualized, as in the Vlinderhof in the Maximapark in Utrecht. His choices for woody plants are always interesting, and there is a feeling he would do more in this line if clients wanted him to.

The only rival in terms of sophistication of technique and commercial success has been the Mixed Planting system developed in Germany, where since the 1980s planting has become increasingly systematized using a very similar palette of plants, with much effort going into the development of mixes of perennials that can be randomized in order to achieve a naturalistic effect. It is significant that Piet has not on the whole gone down this road, although he has experimented with it; he believes the resulting complexity of the plantings makes maintenance more difficult. In some settings, however, usually where he is confident of good ongoing management, he has done so – as with the High Line, where the planting is very complex.

01
Anja and Piet Oudolf.

02
Symphyotrichum 'Twilight' on the former Rotterdam waterfront (Westerkade).

03
Repeating clumps of tufted hair grass (*Deschampsia cespitosa*) are a frequent motif.

04
Hylotelephium 'Matrona' towards the end of its flowering period.

05
Blocks of perennials have always been central to the Oudolf style.

04

05

01

02

Back in the 1990s, the contemporary perennial movement that Piet was a part of reacted to some extent against the widespread use of bedding plants and garish annuals. Over the years, the range of available annuals has changed enormously, with many more varieties in subtle colours or with natural flower shapes. To the surprise of some of his admirers, Piet has very occasionally used them, as in the gardens of Museum Voorlinden at Wassenaar and Noma restaurant in Copenhagen. They are particularly useful to create interest in the first year of planting before the perennials have fully established.

An innovation which is a variant of the randomized intermingling approach is 'matrix plantings', where one relatively low-key species, usually a grass, is used to create a matrix, dominating the ground layer and usually acting as a groundcover, with a variety of other plants more or less randomly dropped into it. This is a good example of the kind of thinking that potentially has very wide application, as it serves a practical function of helping to suppress weeds and cover the soil, as well as an aesthetic one – a background for the stronger colours and shapes of the plants added into the mix.

Another innovation which adds spice to Piet's planting style is the use of 'scatter plants' – varieties that are chosen for a short but prominent period of interest (usually the flowering period) but are relatively inconspicuous before and afterwards. This is a way of adding an apparently spontaneous element for limited periods, as if the plants had seeded themselves in place naturally.

Piet's example has been a global inspiration for a younger generation of designers and plantspeople. The Netherlands may have exported tulips and a vast amount of other nursery-grown plant material, but it has never before exported such a strong idea in planting or garden design. With gardeners and designers as far apart as Patagonia and Hokkaido paying close attention to his work, Dutch planting design has gone truly global.

03

04

01
Planting at Museum
Voorlinden, Wassenaar.

02
Mixing dahlias in with
perennials is a new ploy.

03
Echinacea pallida, one
of the perennials Piet has
used for many years.

04
Dahlias and other
summer flowers blended
with feathertop grass
(*Pennisetum villosum*).

05
Seedheads and dahlias –
a radical new step.

05

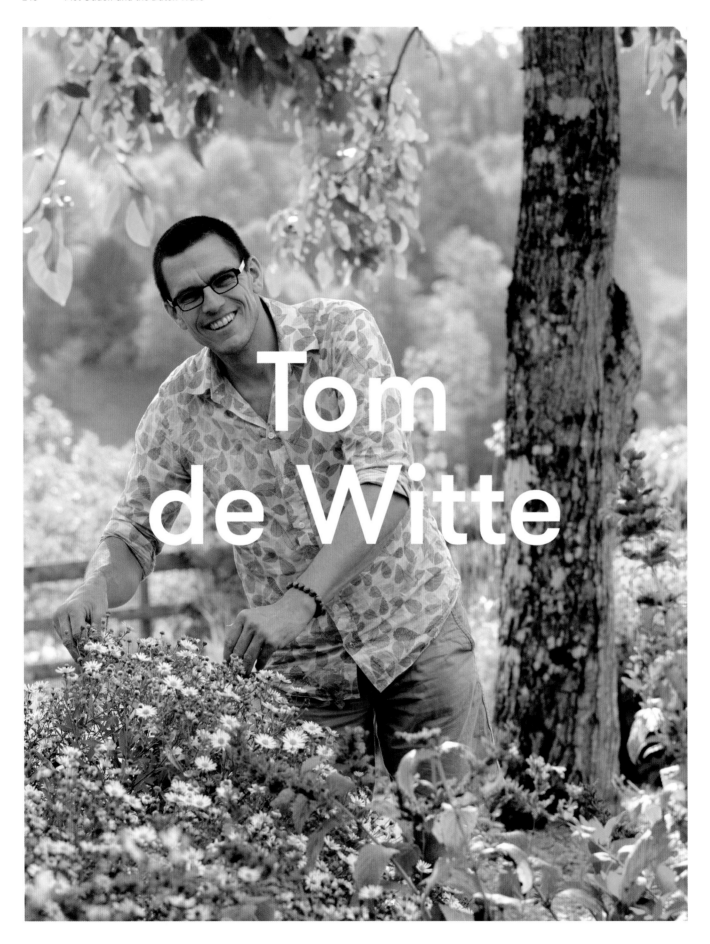

Tom
de Witte

The story of how Tom de Witte first met Piet Oudolf is one of those memories that is sure to go into contemporary garden legend. 'I was 18 and had just passed my driving test,' he recalls. 'I borrowed my mum's car to drive up to Hummelo, I think in 1996 – it was a long way, three and a half hours, and of course no sat-nav in those days, it was all maps.' Home was, and still is, the far south-western corner of the country, in Zeeland, and Hummelo was a long way, particularly for someone who had only just been allowed out onto the roads unaccompanied for the first time. Tom had seen Piet's work when his mother had shown him an article in a gardening magazine. 'I had started gardening at my grandparents' home,' he says 'and I had my own garden at home. It kept growing and growing and when I was 15 or so, I persuaded my parents to let me do a make-over of the whole garden.'

He recalls how, before leaving home, he did gardening for people in the neighbourhood, using a little Renault hatchback car to drive plants and tools round to his clients. He had decided some time earlier that he wanted to be a garden designer, but felt he should start by learning as many practical skills as he could, so when he left school at 17 he took a course in garden and landscape construction at The Horticulture College of Boskoop. He went on to do a three-year course in Garden Architecture at The Royal Academy of Fine Arts in Ghent, Belgium, so by the end he had had seven years of training. Setting up in business as soon as he graduated in 2000, he had already done some work with Piet, who had asked him to help administer plant lists. This was the period when Piet and Anja were running the Grass Days at Hummelo, which Tom says he always attended. 'They were legendary,' he recalls, 'the most important day of the year when all the key people from the plant world got together. They were a catalyst for my career.'

01

02

He also does some design work on specific areas within guidelines discussed with Piet, acting as one of several garden and landscape designers who work with Piet to help him implement his planting design projects.

Tom has his own thriving garden design career too, mostly in The Netherlands, but he has created some gardens in France and, surprisingly, in Japan.

An invitation to participate in the Japan Flower & Garden Show came through Yuko Tanabe, who was then Head Gardener at Huis ten Bosch, a Dutch theme park in Nagasaki in southern Japan, and Tom made a show garden there in 2015. 'It was a good way in,' he says. 'I got to know so many people, and gained clients in Tokyo who asked me to design a roof garden of 700 square metres (837 sq yd).' Designing and supervising the construction of the garden and overseeing its development meant around 15 trips to Japan. Other Japanese projects have followed. Plant availability can be problematic, partly because of language problems and the very different way plant markets operate, so he has to always work through other people. 'We found a good nursery in Hokkaido, but the climate in Tokyo is so different,' he says. For his perennial selection he has to bear in mind hot humid summers as well as plant availability, and the fact that 'the Japanese take the time to achieve a good result and as good planting takes its time as well, it is a slow process'.

An annual event that the Oudolfs had started in the early 1990s, the Grass Days were held over two weekends in September and October, and although they were ostensibly about promoting ornamental grasses, they were also key social occasions for the very collegiate 'new perennial' crowd of gardeners, nursery owners, designers and others.

Part of Tom's work is to collaborate with Piet on projects both at home and in the USA; some of this is project management. 'I am the one who talks to the contractor about things like soil preparation and to the local landscape construction people about getting the plants. Very often I am his ears and eyes on site, and very often I do the laying out of the plants too.'

03

04

05

01
Planting in beds that are
to be seen from all angles.

02
Echinacea pallida makes a
good cut flower.

03
Kalimeris incisa 'Blue Star'
makes a fine late-season
splash.

04
Euphorbia polychroma,
Amsonia hubrichtii,
Eremurus × isabellinus
Ruiter hybrids, *Allium
hollandicum* 'Purple
Sensation', *Achillea
filipendula* 'Gold Plate',
Stipa sp.

05
The swathe of yellow
in this planting is
Rudbeckia fulgida.

01

Tom spends more time talking about the whole garden design environment than most designers do. Many of the gardens he deals with are relatively small and inevitably have problems with the need to screen. A judicious use of woody plants can achieve this and if there are neighbouring elements that are attractive, for example trees, they can be borrowed, in the Japanese sense of the term, while screening out the less desirable elements. This can only happen if the boundary itself is obscured in some way. He has also used pergolas – simple metal framing structures that can be surprisingly effective at creating a distraction in an urban setting and also give a sense of containing and defining the garden space. In rural areas, belts of meadow grass are an effective linking to the surroundings, especially if they also blur the boundaries; informally shaped beds rather than formal ones help ease such transitions. Pointing out something that many regard as a weak point in contemporary naturalistic planting design, Tom says, 'There is a dramatic change in volume when you cut everything down in late winter. It means that the background and framework are now very important – there is nothing else to look at, until the first bulbs and very early perennials begin to show.'

Tom feels that clients should always be encouraged to go out into the garden every day to see if anything new has happened. 'They need stopping places,' he says, 'so I do things like widening a path to make a place for a seat, or creating a situation where they will look at the garden from a different angle.'

02

03

04

This desire for identifying places to stop is perhaps part of what Maayke de Ridder, the very perceptive photographer and partner in creating this book, identifies as 'surprises', although Tom himself says he does not consciously plan these. The appearance of a steel pergola, an unexpected path, a section of the garden with only hedges and no perennials, a ceramic water bowl, can all just slightly jolt the mind from the path of the predictable.

Like an increasing number of designers, Tom is fond of using multi-stem trees as they do not grow so tall, which in some situations can be an advantage, such as urban locations where taller trees might block views or be particularly subject to wind damage. Multiple stems with their tendency to arch outwards create a more

complex and often more natural-feeling visual environment, while Tom feels that the relatively low and dense foliage canopy can act almost as a ceiling, creating the sense of being in a woodland.

A garden in a property which Tom rented some years ago is a masterclass in how to make the most of a difficult site. 'It was what we call a pipeline garden,' he says, meaning long and thin, 'but it does offer the opportunity to create multiple sub-gardens, one after another in a line – so exploring the garden is now very much a journey.' Creating a journey in even the smallest space is vital, he thinks, and if possible providing more than one route to the same space or making it possible to view a planting from more than one angle; he rejects the classical planting at the side

01
Large *Miscanthus* grasses are strong focal points in the plantings.

02
Strong tree and perennial shapes.

03
Actaea simplex Atropurpurea Group 'James Compton', a late-flowering perennial for light shade.

04
Deep purple *Geranium wlassovianum*.

01

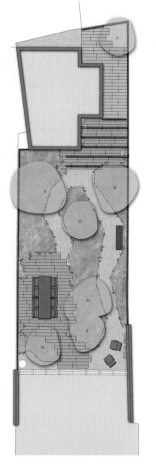

02

03

01
A small garden near the Belgian border.

02
The plan of the garden.

03
Hakonechloa macra is a very distinguished grass that slowly forms clumps.

04
Low-growing plants make an easy transition in a slate-fragment path.

05
Persicaria amplexicaulis 'Blackfield'.

06
Deep red *Hylotelephium telephium* Atropurpureum Group 'Arthur Branch'.

07
Paths weaving in and out maximize the way of exploring the garden.

04

05

06

07

01

03

02

04

05

06

with a central walkway if there is enough space to have a path on either side of the planting. Of his former home, he says, 'It was so much easier to blur the end than if it had been a wide, shallow garden where the boundary is right in front of you.'

Tom advises the repetition of materials in awkward spaces, since having points of continuity is important; this might be a hard element such as paving or a repeated plant. Journeys can be slowed by having as many places to stop as possible: 'They will help you to see the garden from different angles, give you multiple viewpoints, which always work to make a garden look bigger,' he says. The use of hedging cutting into the main axis from the side, forming coulisse-type screens, creates a sense of mystery.

Tom uses a very similar range of plants to Piet and in proportions which are also very similar. However, while Piet's commissions are now almost inevitably large-scale, Tom's are smaller, which means that he cannot be anything like as experimental in the way he puts plants together. The smaller the space, the more important it is that everything in it is in just the right place to maximize impact and is as attractive as possible for as long as possible. Plant juxtapositions have to work, and odd spaces such as corners especially have to be filled with just the right plant. 'Piet can use matrix planting or create mixes, but that is much more difficult in a medium-sized private garden,' Tom says. 'They only work in large spaces, while in smaller gardens you do need to work in groups. Matrix planting involves

limiting the range of species, which is not appropriate for a smaller garden space.'

Where Tom can be more experimental is in the selection of plants. He likes to try new plants in gardens, but 'it has to be led by the clients – there are those who want a garden that works 100 per cent and do not care to take any risks, but in other gardens I try to include small quantities of species I am less familiar with, to treat the garden as a laboratory. I never use big multiples of unknown plants, though, as that is too big a risk.' Although he has always actively gardened, to have experience of all the plants he uses is impossible, so researching plants and then evaluating them over time is important. 'When I use new plants, I check with multiple sources. You can never rely on

07

08

09

10

11

12

what one nursery says, as they will have grown the plants only on one type of soil, so I look at different sources online – but plants don't read books or see the internet, and sometimes they do things you might not expect. I like seeing plants in nature, as sometimes you find them growing in situations you would not predict from where you have seen them grown in gardens.' Of course, for a garden designer such as Tom today, moving forwards means reacting to new varieties in the marketplace but also making plant selections for climate change, finding more species that can survive both occasional flooding and drought, and also satisfying increasing interest from clients in biodiversity and using native plants.

01
Bamboo
Chusquea culeou.

02
Clipped beeches create an atmosphere of intrigue.

03
The flowers of
Heptacodium miconioides.

04
Aquilegia vulgaris flowers in Tom's former long and narrow garden.

05
Geranium 'Ann Thompson' and *Hakonechloa macra.*

06
Detail of the flowers of *Molopospermum peloponnesiacum*

07
Persicaria amplexicaulis 'Blackfield'; the tree is *Albizia lophantha.*

08
The seedheads of
Molopospermum peloponnesiacum.

09
Acer griseum, a tree for a sheltered location.

10
Lacy *Molopospermum* against beech hedging.

11
Tetradium daniellii, a small tree, with the dark foliage of *Actaea simplex* Atropurpurea Group 'James Compton'.

12
The seedheads of
Astrantia major.

Why a book about Dutch gardens?
Noel Kingsbury

The year of 1994 was one in which I spent a lot of time travelling, looking at gardens in Brazil, Germany and finally, in August, going to meet Piet Oudolf at his garden in Hummelo for the first time. I have been back almost every year since. I was initially attracted by the passion of those involved in naturalistic planting, trying to capture the beauty of wild vegetation in parks, planting wild flowers in gardens, integrating spaces for wildlife and using recycled materials, but I soon discovered so much more.

Despite the many similarities between this country and Britain (climate and the range of plants grown, to say nothing of history and culture), I felt there were subtle but distinct differences between our two garden cultures; put me in a Dutch garden and I know almost instantly that I am in The Netherlands and not back in the UK. That difference was the start of this book.

In the intervening years I have visited all sorts of Dutch gardens, from the historic to the boldly contemporary, the formal to the wild, the disciplined to the anarchic, and a range of community gardens, but I have also looked at planting in a wide range of public spaces: parks, roadsides and corporate landscapes. There is great diversity, but many common themes too, and with the huge growth of interest in garden design over the last few years, now is a good time to look at how garden designers are responding to the inspiration not only of the landscape but also of a rich garden history.

Meeting some extraordinary and inspirational people was an important part of the story too – Piet Oudolf and his wife Anja, for a start. Two, sadly, are no longer with us: one is Henk Gerritsen, whom I met on my first visit to Piet, when he took me to visit Henk's Priona Gardens. Henk was an artist, a maker of gardens, an enthusiast for nature and a superb writer on the subject of plants and natural vegetation. The other is Rob Leopold, a philosopher and entrepreneur, whose engaging personal style made him a natural and highly effective networker.

Travelling of any kind involves a potential engagement with landscape. For me, this soon became more than simply driving or riding through it in the train. The Dutch landscape at first appears very uniform, even at times monotonous, but over time it begins to reveal its subtleties and secrets.

Beneath those big skies is a created landscape, shaped over centuries; I became increasingly fascinated by how much and how frequently it had changed over time.

Historic maps normally show a gradual cumulative increase in places, roads and names over time, but here they showed wholesale land reorganization: lakes and areas of the sea disappearing, islands appearing and sometimes vanishing, rivers changing course, often multiple times, connecting, disconnecting, or being lost. What at first sight seemed to be a

featureless landscape nearly always held clues to its past: dykes that suddenly ended, random bends in roads, and odd corners with scrub and rough grass. I began to realize the fascination of a landscape that owed its current form to layer upon layer of reshaping, much as a garden is so often a tapestry of the different plannings and plantings of several generations.

The making and setting out of gardens, and of planting in particular, has been at the core of my professional life, so using gardens as a route into looking at a foreign but at the same time oddly familiar country and culture seemed a good way of exploring this country's landscape history – and so it turned out to be.

Why a book about Dutch gardens?
Maayke de Ridder

Over the years, as a garden photographer, I have visited and admired many gardens in and outside The Netherlands, not only gardens made by private individuals, but also those designed by professional garden designers and landscape architects. In travelling around the world I saw many different ways of making gardens, as each country has its own particular style. However I honestly felt that the Dutch way of making gardens distinguishes itself really clearly from the others by its clarity of form and its desire to embrace the contemporary.

The Netherlands undoubtedly has numerous talents in many fields of design. In interiors, 'Dutch Design' is a global brand, while in gardening we have had the 'New Perennial Movement', which has even been dubbed the 'Dutch Wave'. Since roughly the beginning of the last century, we have had a number of progressive garden and landscape designers of world renown, and in recent decades, we have seen many more, all inspired by their predecessors, but often also by the landscape in which, and with which, they work. What strikes me most about them is the very high quality and the diversity of that work.

The Netherlands is a small and densely populated country, so many designers start by designing small gardens – indeed what we Dutch consider a huge garden would often be regarded as a small one in neighbouring countries. And so the Dutch have definitely become masters of small-garden design! This is more difficult than designing a large garden – everything has to balance and every part has to look good. What is special, perhaps, is that many of these designers don't necessarily turn their hand to larger ones as their career progresses, as will be clear in this book, but stay loyal to 'small is beautiful' – and as private individuals are increasingly opting for a designer garden, attaching greater importance to an atmosphere of greenery around the house, their loyalty is rewarded.

Novice designers often receive their first assignments from garden owners in their own neighbourhood – sometimes they continue working primarily locally, whereas others may design in other parts of the country. Soil type plays an important role in developing a design, but the character of the landscape does as well. This is something that particularly interests me, and I had been planning to make a book about the influence of landscape on garden design for some time. In a conversation with publisher Hélène Lesger, it turned out that she had also wanted to make a book about the connections between the Dutch landscape and gardens. So, the starting point of the book was quickly established: linking a designer to a different aspect of the landscape.

Our landscapes and their histories, all of them cultivated and shaped often over hundreds of years, have always fascinated me. However, many Dutch people find their countryside boring and only become enthusiastic about a landscape when they think of England, France or Italy. But the Netherlands is beautiful and very diverse, although sometimes you may have to be observant and pay attention to the details.

While walking or driving through the country, I have seen some fantastic places, products of culture and of nature – not only the impressive ones such as the Afsluitdijk, the Houtribdijk or the Delta Works, but also gems such as the landscape of Northeast Groningen, the Weerribben, the Ellertsveld, the Posbank, the Land van Maas and Waal or the Verdronken Land van Saeftinghe. It is also fun to hear or read stories and legends about these sometimes mysterious landscapes.

So here we look at garden designers in the context of various aspects of Dutch natural and cultural landscapes – firstly at those landscapes that are the products of many centuries of human interaction with what nature provided, then at more artificial, more planned and organized, but always functional landscapes, and finally at landscapes created to please the eye and provide habitat for humanity.

An extra dimension is added because the book is written by an English author, Noel Kingsbury, who has embraced the Dutch landscape and the work of Dutch garden architects. I hope it offers a surprising and refreshing view of our country and of those designers who shape its gardens and public spaces.

Bold numerals refer to images.

LANDSCAPE ARCHITECTS

Carolien Barkman
www.carolienbarkman.nl

Arjan Boekel
Boekel Tuin en Landschap
www.boekeltuinen.nl

Robert Broekema
Buro Robert Broekema
www.robert-broekema.nl

Monique Donders and Pierre
van der Heiden
Donders! & van der Heiden
www.denkersintuinen.nl

Luc Engelhard
Architectuur in buitenruimte
www.lucengelhard.nl

Jacqueline van der Kloet
Jacqueline van der Kloet tuinontwerp
en beplantingsadvies
www.theetuin.nl/jacquelinevanderkloet

Nico Kloppenborg
www.nicokloppenborg.nl

Frank van der Linden
Van Nature Tuinarchitectuur
www.vannaturetuinarchitectuur.nl

Noël van Mierlo
Van Mierlo Tuinen
www.vanmierlotuinen.nl

Emiel Versluis & Margo van Beem
Vis á Vis Ontwerpers
www.visavisontwerpers.nl

Machiel Vlieland
Extra Vert
www.extravert.nl

Tom de Witte
www.tomdewitte.com

GARDENS TO VISIT

The landscapes in this book are of
course free to visit. In addition the
gardens listed below are open to the
public. Please check for information
on the website before setting out.

Keukenhof
www.keukenhof.nl

De Theetuin
www.theetuin.nl

Paleis Het Loo
www.paleishetloo.nl

Jac. P. Thijssepark
www.thijssepark.nl

Tuinen Mien Ruys
www.tuinenmienruys.nl

PHOTO CREDITS

All photos by Maayke de Ridder except for
those listed below.

beeldbank.rws.nl, Rijkswaterstaat:
p 16/17
Buro Mien Ruys:
p 222 01, 02, 03, 04
DelanoBalten Visuals/Shutterstock.com:
p 157 08
Donaldb/Shutterstock.com:
p 141 04
easy.dans.knaw.nl/ui/datasets/id/easy-
dataset:75437:
p 11 01
Elizabeth Whiting & Associates/Alamy
Stock Photo:
p 116
Hanneke Reijbroek:
p 153 02, 03, 05
kwaad.net/Purmerend-Geschiedenis.html:
p 20 01
p 79 07
Lamtasweer/Shutterstock.com:
p 100 02, 03, 04
Maaike Kampert Fotografie:
p 142
Modeste Herwig:
p 242 01
Paleis Het Loo, Apeldoorn:
p 176
puc.overheid.nl:
p 121 01, 02, 03, 04
p 121 02
p 156 01
Rijksmuseum Amsterdam:
p 13 03
p 20 02
p 39 01, 02, 03
p 78 05
p 79 08, 09
p 102 01, 02, 03
p 103 04, 05
p 140 01
p 141 06
p 178 01, 02, 03, 04
p 179 05
Stadsarchief Amsterdam:
P 196

ACKNOWLEDGEMENTS

We would like to thank all the garden designers who collaborated with us on this book in telling their stories, explaining their methods and revealing their inspirations. And of course all the owners of gardens they have designed who generously allowed their gardens to be photographed: Family Akinci-Beunen, Akker-van der Veen, Van Amsterdam, Barneveld, Brouwel, Van der Burg, Douqué, Eeftingh, Entjes-de Kruijf, Van Erp, Gooskens-Schuur, Jacobs, Keuning-Nikkessen, Kleisterlee, Kuiper, Lodeizen, Long, Van Marwijk, Oudshoorn-Nijs, Ploegmakers, Van Pul, Schäfer, Scherbeijn-van de Voorde, Skura, van der Ven, Van der Vleuten, Van de Voorde.

We would also like to thank the staff of those public gardens and parks we have featured: Tuinen Mien Ruys, Het Loo, Jac. P. Thijssepark, de Theetuin and Keukenhof; and friends and colleagues whom we have discussed the project with: Piet Oudolf, Leo den Dulk and Ruurd van Donkelaar. We are grateful to the designer, Alan Watt, for making this a very special book visually, especially given the range of material we presented him with. And finally a very special thanks to Hélène Lesger for being part of this dream of a project, seeing its potential and making it happen; it has needed insight and patience, two qualities she combines so well.

Maayke de Ridder and Noel Kingsbury